THE FRICK COLLECTION

Anshen Transdisciplinary Lectureships in Art, Science and the Philosophy of Culture

---

MONOGRAPH THREE

Previously Published:

MONOGRAPH ONE
THE REAL DISCOVERY OF AMERICA:
MEXICO, NOVEMBER 8, 1519
by
Hugh Thomas

MONOGRAPH TWO
THE ORIGIN OF THE UNIVERSE
AND THE ORIGIN OF RELIGION
by
Sir Fred Hoyle

LANGUAGE AND THOUGHT

by Noam Chomsky

MOYER BELL

WAKEFIELD, RHODE ISLAND & LONDON

Published by Moyer Bell

First Edition

LIBRARY OF CONGRESS
CATALOGING-IN-PUBLICATION DATA

Chomsky, Noam.
    Language and thought / by Noam Chomsky. — 1st ed.
        p. cm. — (Anshen transdisciplinary lectureships in art, science, and the philosophy of culture : monograph 3)
Includes bibliographical references (p.).
    1. Psycholinguistics. 2. Language and languages—Philosopy. 3. Thought and thinking. I. Title. II. Series.
P37.C546   1994
401′.9—dc20   93-36148
                                              CIP
    ISBN 1-55921-074-5 (cl) 1994
    ISBN 1-55921-076-1 (pb) 1995

Printed in the United States of America
Distributed in North America by Publishers Group West, P.O. Box 8843, Emeryville CA 94662 800-788-3123 (in California 510-658-3453) and in Europe by Gazelle Book Services Ltd., Falcon House, Queen Square, Lancaster LA1 1RN England 524-68765.

CONTENTS

INTRODUCTION

On the occasion of this third Anshen Transdisciplinary Lecture in Art, Science, and the Philosophy of Culture, I am pleased to welcome you to The Frick Collection. It is an honor to greet you on behalf of our Trustees and our staff. Once again we are drawn by Dr. Ruth Anshen's remarkable vision, this time to explore questions of language and thought with one of the most celebrated, most provocative thinkers of our age. Dr. Noam Chomsky has frequently challenged us in his discussions of contemporary social and political behavior. He remains a foremost challenger regarding questions of language and linguistics, and he no doubt will provide a forthright and invigorating investigation tonight.

In order to facilitate the discussion following Dr. Chomsky's talk, we have gathered on the stage several persons who will reply to him. The leader of this discussion will be Dr. Eric Wanner, president of the Russell Sage Foundation, a distinguished scholar of cognitive science and a leader in various programs concerning behavioral sciences. He will be joined by three professors who are also present on the platform with us: Dr. Akeel Bilgrami, Professor of Philosophy at Columbia University; Dr. George Miller, Professor of Psychology at Princeton University; and Dr. James Schwartz, Professor of Neurology at the College of Physicians and Surgeons, Columbia University, also well known as a philosopher and a linguist.

The first two lectures in this series are already in print: one by Lord Hugh Thomas, who spoke about *The Real Discovery of America*; and Sir Fred Hoyle's talk on *The Origin of the Universe and the Origin of Religion*, given a year ago, on April 2, 1992, which has just been published. Dr. Anshen has guided these transdisciplinary lectures with indefatigable concern for every part of the process. Her own most recent book, *Morals Equals Manners*, was also published within the year, and has been received widely with acclaim. She has been at the heart of all the planning for this evening. Philosophy, mathematics, the sciences generally are held in her life with the same kind of grace, knowledge, intuition, and quickness of mind as are history, the social sciences, art, and music. Ruth Anshen is a rare—no, a unique—bearer in our own time of the ancient Greek spirit, of the Greek philosophical soul. We are most happy to have her open our proceedings today.

—Charles Ryskamp

PREFACE

Since we are all plunged in language, necessity is laid upon me to say the following few words;

If any single concern distinguishes present scholars in all disciplines, it is a concentration of attention upon language, but only in each isolated discipline. Convinced as I am, some of our worst contemporary muddles are due to the general neglect of language as an instrument of thought.

Language is far too interesting and important to be left to the old-line philologist or contemporary reductionist. For there is a unity that springs from two assumptions. One is that the connection between the human psyche and speech is far more subtle and complicated than one realizes. The other is that language, though it is but one of the ways by which we communicate with each other, conveys not only thought but also emotion, so that a merely rational analysis of language will no more explain it than a chemical explanation of a rose will define the rose.

Those of us who are lovers of words, to whom a fine phrase brings a blush of response, know that words are merely one medium through which we express our crying out, our salutation, our discovery and our assent to what happens to us from within and to what happens to us from without. Like all lovers we add as much as we can to what we love. We are not lovers for nothing, but for life itself. I will tell you a short story:

Tormented by a spiritual thirst a traveller who was a Prophet wandered in a gloomy desert when an angel appeared to him at the cross-road and cried, "Arise, Prophet, and go over land and sea and *emblazone* the hearts of people with a *Word.*" (So wrote Pushkin, the Russian poet.) And as that ancient Greek Epitome of wisdom, Heraclitus, said "Do not listen to me but to the Word."

Thought itself must be accompanied by a critical understanding of the relation of linguistic expression to the deeper and most persistent intuition of man. It is by virtue of the provocative power of language which grasps, shakes, and transforms that human beings become human. For nothing really human can be so without this meaning, whether the language be uttered or silent. In this way, language as the power of universals is given to us in order that we must transcend our environment, in order that we may have a world. Thus, we are thrust into a state of universal mobility since we attach the swift and restless force of our individual existence to the retarded and more massive power of language. And for this there is only one source, namely, the very nature of mind.

If words issued from an origin other than mind, from one's native land, one's country, they would be born and they would die with it. Thus we would be deceived, tricked into an illusion.

The problem of this wondrous gift which enables us to communicate with others, to reveal to others the hidden secrets of our being, to invoke the psychical properties of the mind and heart in invocation, expressing our sorrows, in grief, or despair, in entreaty through this unique instrument, language, which entrusted to the written or spoken tradition defeats the voracity of time. This is the problem concerning us, taxing our minds and our hearts. It is language, full-panoplied, and alive, issuing hot and pulsating from the human mouth; it is language severed from all practical, all immediate applicability which teaches us that words are the ultimate symbols of ideas and that the power of life or death lies in the tongue.

The word is power. And it is power precisely because it awakens to life secret and latent forces. Its work is that of evoking powers hitherto hidden or inert but awaiting only that summons to bring them into the light, to reveal them, to foster their entrance into existence and into time. Such was the power that, from the very inception of civilization, man has attributed to the word.

Language is a process of liberation from conceptual, logical or discursive rationalism. Language not only articulates, connects and infers, it also envisages, and the intuitive grasping of language is the primary act and function of that one and single power which is called reason. For it is then that we may pass from the passive acceptance of sense-data to a fresh, constructive, and spontaneous insight into the universe. Language thus becomes indispensable not only for the construction of the world of thought but also for the construction of the world of perception, both of which constitute the ultimate nexus of an intelligible communion, spiritual and moral, between all of us.

Language is an energy, an activity, not only of communication and self-expression but of orientation in the universe. It is the spirit made flesh. The violent muteness, the desperate isolation we experience finally breaks through in language. And it is the creation of ever-widening horizons of human communication which is now coming to embrace all humanity that we are summoned by an unbending inner necessity to nourish and honor—the vision of communication through communion. We need not seek the word; the word is given within us.

And finally, we remember, as Wilhelm von Humboldt, that great philosopher of language, has said, "We are human not because we have language but because we *are* language."

—Ruth Nanda Anshen

LANGUAGE AND THOUGHT

LANGUAGE AND THOUGHT

Let me quickly allay any expectations that I might hope to do more than chip away at the rather grandiose themes suggested by the title of these remarks. The themes go back to the origins of recorded thought, and reach to the heart of our nature. They have elicited intricate and subtle inquiry, accelerating in recent years. The empirically-oriented disciplines concerned with language and thinking have become highly specialized. When I was a graduate student forty years ago, it took no great effort to master the theoretical content of linguistics and psychology; what was then at all understood occupies very little of today's curricula. Not many years ago, every faculty member in my own department could take an active part in every thesis defense. Those days are long past.

Specialization is no proof of progress; it has often meant displacement of penetrating insights in favor of technical manipulation of little interest. That remains partially true today, in my opinion, though only partially.

Traditional questions are no longer forgotten or dismissed as absurd and senseless, as they were during the heyday of "behavioral science" and the various brands of structuralism. They have been reopened and in some cases, seriously investigated. New questions are being posed that could not have been imagined a few years ago, and they seem to be the right ones, opening the way to new understanding, and unsuspected problems. There has been explosive growth in the range of empirical phenomena that are reasonably well understood, and to which explanatory theory must be answerable.

Similar evaluations were given in the past, incorrectly in my view. They should be regarded with a skeptical eye today as well. Even in the case of work of considerable care and sophistication, it may be useful to recall Voltaire's thoughts about metaphysics: a dance with elegant moves, but you end up where you started. The gap between public relations success and relevant achievement often seems to me rather impressive; I have in mind claims about the enormous promise of neural net (connectionist) models or artificial intelligence, or about a "cognitive revolution." Nevertheless, in some areas progress has been significant, I think.

I will try to sketch the landscape as it looks to me, stressing in advance that it is a personal and surely a minority view.

A standard starting point is the framework constructed by Gottlob Frege just a hundred years ago, which has proved a paradigm for much that followed. Frege's basic assumption is that "mankind possesses a common treasure of thoughts which is transmitted from generation to generation," something that "cannot well be denied." Were it not the case, "a common science would be impossible." These common thoughts are expressed in a shared public language, consisting of shared signs. A sign has two aspects. First, it designates an object in the world, its referent; in a "logically perfect language," that will be true for every "well constructed" expression. Second, a sign has a "sense" that fixes the reference and is "grasped by everybody" who knows the language; to understand an expression is to know its sense in the shared public language. In addition, each person may have an individual mental image connected with the objective sense. Sign, sense, and referent are external entities, outside the mind/brain. To adopt Frege's analogy, suppose that we observe the moon through a telescope. We may think of the real image of the moon projected in the interior of the telescope, an object common to all observers, as analogous to the sense; the individual retinal image is analogous to the individual mental image.

The basic picture has been widely adopted. The idea that a sign picks out an object in the world to which it refers "makes evident good sense," Gareth Evans observes in one of the most important recent studies of reference. It has occasionally been questioned, for example, by Peter Strawson, who warned 40 years ago of "the myth of the logically proper name," to which we may add related beliefs about indexicals and pronouns. In very recent work, Akeel Bilgrami develops an account in terms of agents' conceptions with a much narrower dependence on external object and shared public language. But such qualms are rare, and may not go far enough.

The Fregean picture has technical problems that have inspired a great deal of insightful work, but it is worth noting that none of its principles is obvious. The issues that arise are too intricate and wide-ranging to hope to review. Let me simply indicate a few doubts.

The basic assumption that there is a common store of thoughts surely *can* be denied; in fact, it *had* been plausibly denied a century earlier by critics of the theory of ideas who argued that it is a mistake to interpret the expression "John has a thought" (desire, intention, etc.) on the analogy of "John has a diamond." In the former case, the encyclopedist du Marsais and later Thomas Reid argued, the expression means only "John thinks" (desires, etc.), and provides no grounds for positing "thoughts" to which John stands in a relation. To say that people have similar thoughts is to say that they think alike, perhaps so much alike that we even say they have the same thought, as we say that two people live in the same place. But from this we cannot move to saying that there are thoughts that they share, or a store of such thoughts. Philosophers have been misled by the "surface grammar" of a "systematically misleading expression," to adopt terms introduced when this " ordinary language" approach was reinvented 150 years later. Argument is required to show that thoughts are entities that are "possessed," as diamonds are. How solid the argument is may be questioned, in my opinion.

Consider the second assumption: that the shared thoughts are expressed in a "common public language." Some version of this idea is presupposed by virtually all work in philosophy of language and philosophical semantics. Many would agree with Michael Dummett, incidentally a leading Frege scholar, that you and I not only share a public language, but that that language —English—exists "independently of any particular speakers"; each of us has only a "partial, and partially erroneous, grasp of the language." This idea is completely foreign to the empirical study of language. Nor has anyone ever indicated what sense it might have; how do we decide, for example, whether the word "disinterested" in the language I partially know is pronounced as in Boston or in Oxford, or whether it means *uninterested*, as almost all speakers believe (ignorantly, we are told), or *unbiased*, as certain authority figures insist? For the empirical study of language, the questions are meaningless. What are called "languages" or "dialects" in ordinary usage are complex amalgams determined by colors on maps, oceans, political institutions, and so on, with obscure normative-teleological aspects. And there is no theoretical construct to replace them, or explanatory gap that such a construct might fill if it were devised. It is true that Peter and Mary may talk alike, while neither talks like Deng Xiaoping. Similarly, they may look alike and live near one another, though neither looks like or lives near Deng. From these facts, we do not conclude that there are common shapes that people share, or that the world is divided into objective areas, even as idealizations; or languages and communities to which these languages belong.

To ask whether Peter speaks the same language as Mary is like asking whether Boston is near New York but not London, or whether John is almost home, except that the dimensionality provided by interest and circumstance is far more diverse and complex. In ordinary human life, we find all sorts of shifting communities and expectations, varying widely with individuals and groups, and no "right answer" as to how they should be selected. People also enter into various and shifting authority and deference relations. The problem is not one of vagueness; rather, of hopeless underspecification. It is not a matter of abstraction from diversity, any more than in the case of "near Boston" or "looks like"; rather, there is no general way to abstract, though given particular interests we can, as when we say that the language of southern Sweden was once Danish but became Swedish a few years later without changing, as a result of military conquest. Such informal notions as Swedish-vs.-Danish, norms and conventions, or misuse of language are generally unproblematic under conditions of normal usage, as is "near New York" or "looks like Mary." But they can hardly be expected to enter into attempts to reach theoretical understanding. A good deal of the most serious work in the study of meaning and intentionality relies uncritically on such notions, and must be seriously reconsidered, in my opinion.

It is commonly assumed that such notions must be invoked to account for "rule-following" and for the fact of communication. Thus rule-following can be attributed only when there are standards of "*correctness* of use or application in terms of *common agreement in linguistic practice*, a shared form of life," a practice in a shared community language, as Strawson puts the Wittgensteinian point in his 1983 Woodbridge lectures. It is, perhaps, a curiosity that this is a doctrine of "ordinary language philosophy," since ordinary language takes quite a different course. If my granddaughter were to say "I brang the book," we would not hesitate to say she is following the rule for "sing-sang-sung," contrary to "common agreement." True, her internal language may change, replacing "brang" with "brought." If it does not, she'll be speaking a language that differs from mine in this among many other respects, and speaking it "correctly," insofar as the word means anything. Questions of meaning are usually considered different, and somehow more profound. That has to be argued; in fact, they seem merely more obscure, but no different in relevant respects.

We might take note of the doctrine that attribution of rule-following, or mental states and processes generally, requires accessibility to consciousness. This terminological stipulation—it is no more than that—runs counter to common usage, has no place in inquiry into language and thought in the manner of the sciences, and falls onto hopeless problems. The doctrine becomes only more mysterious when supplemented by an unexplained (and, it seems, unintelligible) notion of "access in principle," as in John Searle's recent efforts to avoid obvious problems that have been raised. These matters have been discussed elsewhere; I will not pursue them here.

As for communication, it does not require shared "public meanings" any more than it requires "public pronunciations." Nor need we assume that the "meanings" (or "sounds") of one participant be discoverable by the other. Communication is a more-or-less matter, seeking a fair estimate of what the other person said and has in mind. A reasonable speculation is that we tacitly assume that the other person is identical to us, then introducing modifications as needed, largely reflexively, beyond the level of consciousness. The task may be easy, difficult, or impossible, and accurate determination is rarely required for communication to succeed for the purpose at hand. It could turn out there really is something like "public shared meaning," because the highly restrictive innate properties of the language faculty allow so little variation; that would be an interesting (and not surprising) empirical discovery, but there is no conceptual requirement that anything of the sort be true.

What of Frege's third basic idea, that a sign selects an object in the world, in a manner determined by its sense? Note first that these ideas are not part of ordinary usage; Frege had to invent technical terms, for that reason. That fact does not discredit these moves; theoretical discourse rarely adheres to "folk science." But it does raise questions: are the technical innovations appropriate? True, people use words to refer to things and talk about them, but it is quite a leap to conclude that the *words* refer to these things.

Suppose I tell you, "I had an interview at BBC the other day and was shocked by the deterioration of the city." Someone observing the exchange might say, accurately, that I was referring to and talking about London, though I did not use any word that picks out London by virtue of its meaning (conversely, if I say "London is or is not on the Thames," I may be making a point of logic, not referring to London at all). Furthermore, is there an object London to which I am referring? If so, it is a very curious thing. Thus we allow that under some circumstances, London could be completely destroyed and rebuilt somewhere else 1000 years hence, still being London, that same thing. Charles Dickens described Washington as "the City of Magnificent Intentions," with "spacious avenues, that begin in nothing, and lead nowhere; streets, mile-long, that only want houses , roads, and inhabitants; public buildings that need but a public to be complete and ornaments of great thoroughfares, which only lack great thoroughfares to ornament"—but still Washington. We can regard London with or without regard to its population: from one point of view, it is the same city if its people desert it; from another, we can say that London came to have a harsher feel to it through the Thatcher years, a comment on how people act and live. Referring to London, we can be talking about a location, people who sometimes live there, the air above (but not too high), buildings, institutions, etc., in various combinations. A single occurrence of the term can serve all these functions simultaneously, as when I say that London is so unhappy, ugly, and polluted that it should be destroyed and rebuilt 100 miles away. No object in the world could have this collection of properties.

Such terms as *London* are used to talk about the actual world, but there neither are nor are believed to be things-in-the-world with the properties of the intricate modes of reference that a city name encapsulates; to assume so would quickly lead to extreme paradox. Furthermore, we find much the same wherever we inquire into lexical properties. Suppose I say, "that book, which John wrote in his head, weighs five pounds." The book to which I am referring is simultaneously abstract and concrete, not a thing in the world. In general, a linguistic expression provides a complex perspective from which to think about, talk about, and refer to things, or what we take to be things; the conclusion only becomes clearer as we move from the simplest case—proper names and common nouns—to words with inherent relational structures and more complex constructions. The most elaborate dictionaries provide no more than bare hints about the meanings of words (or about their sounds), just as the most elaborate traditional grammars provide only hints about the form and meaning of complex constructions—hints that may be adequate for a human intelligence, which has the requisite understanding and structures, in large measure independently of experience. My internally stored language, an individual property, provides such perspectives and ways for me to express my thoughts using them; so does yours, and insofar as they are similar, and we are similar in other respects, we can communicate more or less well.

The pervasive property of "poverty of stimulus" is striking even in the case of simple lexical items. Their semantic properties are highly articulated and intricate and known in detail that vastly transcends any relevant experience, and is largely independent of variations of experience and of specific neural structures over a broad range. That conclusion too becomes more firmly established as we move to the meanings of multi-word constructions. To take a very simple example, consider the way we interpret "missing phrases," as in the paired expressions "John ate an apple," "John ate," the latter understood to mean that John ate something or other; here we apply the natural rule that if an expression is "missing," we interpret it to be "something or other." Consider next the sentence, "John is too stubborn to talk to Bill," meaning that John, being stubborn, won't talk to Bill. Suppose we drop "Bill," yielding "John is too stubborn to talk to." Applying the natural rule (i.e., by analogy to the former case), we conclude that this sentence means that John, being stubborn, won't talk to someone or other. But it does not; rather, it means that people won't talk to John (because of his stubbornness). John is being talked to, not doing the talking, and the unspecified person is doing the talking, not being talked to; the interpretations of the former case are inverted.

To illustrate in a slightly more subtle case, consider the sentence "Jones was too angry to run the meeting." Who is understood to be running the meeting? There are two interpretations: The "silent subject" of "run" can be taken to be Jones, so that the meaning is that Jones wouldn't run the meeting because of his anger; in this case we say that the silent subject is "controlled" by *Jones*. Or it can be taken to be unspecified in reference, so that the meaning is that (say) we couldn't run the meeting because of Jones's anger (compare "the crowd was too angry to run the meeting"). Suppose that we replace "the meeting" by a question phrase, so we now have: "which meeting was Jones too angry to run?" Now the ambiguity is resolved; *Jones* refused to run the meeting (compare "which meeting was the crowd too angry to run," interpreted counter-intuitively to mean that the crowd was supposed to run the meeting, unlike "which meeting was the crowd too angry for us to run?"—which has no "silent subject" that requires interpretation).

The reasons are well-understood in such cases as these. The crucial point is that all of this is known without experience and involves computational processes and principles that are quite inaccessible to consciousness, applying to a wide range of phenomena in typologically diverse languages. Even the relevant phenomena had escaped attention until recently, probably because the facts are known "intuitively," as part of our nature, without experience. Serious inquiry begins when we are willing to be surprised by simple phenomena of nature, such as the fact that an apple falls from a tree, or a phrase means what it does. If we are satisfied with the "explanation" that things fall to their natural place or that our knowledge of form and meaning results from experience or perhaps natural selection, then we can be sure that the very phenomena will remain hidden from view, let alone any understanding of what lies behind them.

Such understanding as we have of these matters does

not seem to be enhanced by invoking thoughts that we grasp, public pronunciations or meanings, common languages that we partially know, or a relation of reference between words and things and a mode of fixing it. An "internalist" approach that eschews such obscure notions seems to provide an adequate basis for the study of language and its use, of our interactions with other persons and the external environment. It provides no barrier against skepticism, but there is no reason why it should. Though I won't pursue the issue here, I do not know of any (non-question begging) argument against a full-blown "internalism" of the Cartesian variety that doubts the existence of external things; within this skeptical view, the concepts would (trivially) not be "of external things" and would not arise through experience or evolution. The proposals seem to me of no interest, but also not literally refutable or unintelligible.

In this connection, we may take note of the occasional suggestion that the problem of accounting for language use and acquisition is simplified or solved if we assume that these processes are somehow "based on meaning," the idea being that semantics is soft and mushy, reflecting beliefs and perceptions, goals and interests, community practices, and so on. Thus "semantics-based" approaches will not induce the "crisis" caused by the gap between the apparent rule-governed, algorithmic, digital character of syntax and the apparent variability and continuous flux of individual experience and neural structure; suggestions of Gerald Edelman's are a recent example. Such speculations cannot withstand the most casual look at simple semantic properties, which pose all the same problems as arcane syntactic constructions: they are rule-governed, sharply delineated, and fixed in relative independence of experience and known aspects of neural structure. Furthermore, the problem is seriously misstated. The gap between what is known about language and about the brain sciences or experience is real enough, but it is not a "crisis" or "embarrassment" for cognitive psychology, as sometimes alleged. Rather, it is a typical problem of unification in the sciences: successful explanatory theory at one level cannot be integrated with others, perhaps because the others have to be fundamentally recast. Not many years ago, it was believed that knowledge of language is at most simple induction from extensive experience or even training, and languages appeared to differ from one another as radically as neural structures do to many a trained eye today. That will be true of any complex system, before it comes to be understood, and its principles of organization and function are discovered. That aside, the belief that a semantics-based approach is an alternative to one that is syntax-based derives from misreading of the literature so extreme as to defy brief comment.

Recall that Frege was speaking of a "logically perfect language," one that will allow for "a common science." He regarded natural language as not only imperfect, but even "in principle incoherent," Dummett argues. If so, his specific project is unaffected by any of these considerations. But we may ask what it has to do with the inquiry into language and thought. Perhaps very little. Voltaire's unkind thoughts may not be entirely unfair, adapted to the present case.

Frege's project may be well-designed for his specific purposes. In the enterprise of science and mathematics, one might argue, the goal is to develop a "perfect language" to express a "common treasure of thoughts" with terms that refer to actual things in the world, including natural kinds, understood as the kinds of nature, a concept foreign to natural language. The proposal seems to me to capture the commitments of the working scientist in a reasonable way. In the corner of science in which I work, when I propose a technical concept embedded in a theoretical framework, I mean others to understand that I intend it to refer to something real—typically, some state or property of the brain, ultimately. I presume that in the more central parts of the natural sciences, intentions are similar; when Roger Penrose, say, writes that such mathematical objects as electric and magnetic fields must be understood to be "*real* physical 'stuff'" because of the way they "push each other about," he means what he writes, and uses the term "field" to refer. Pursuing the quest for theoretical understanding, we will not introduce a term such as "London," which can be used to refer in a wide range of perplexing ways, even in a single occurrence. It would be sheer (and unlikely) accident if concepts of language and common sense understanding were to survive the transition to this enterprise.

Suppose we take a Fregean "perfect language" to be a goal of science. Suppose we claim further that science is just refined common sense. Then the Fregean project would indirectly tell us something important about thought and language: it would delineate an ideal to which they approximate, something like a frictionless plane, or so it could be argued.

The reasoning assumes, first, that the symbolic systems constructed for science are languages, merely "more perfect" than human language; and second, that the scientific enterprise that proceeds over generations, leading to the deliberate and painstaking formulation of a system of alleged truths, makes use of the mechanisms of common sense understanding. These assumptions are hardly obvious. Let's consider them in turn.

The child's language "grows in the mind" as the visual system develops the capacity for binocular vision, or as the child undergoes puberty at a certain stage of maturation. Language acquisition is something that happens to a child placed in a certain environment, not something that the child does. The symbolic systems created in the scientific enterprise differ radically from natural languages in their fundamental formal properties, as in their semantic properties, it appears. To call them "language" is simply to adopt a metaphor. We could not draw conclusions about the problems of working Americans by taking the physicist's concept of *work* to be an ideal that is approximated. The move is no more appropriate in the present case. It has led to deep confusion in modern linguistics and philosophy of language resulting from faulty structural analogies between formal systems and natural language; the problems only mount when we turn to questions of meaning and intentionality.

The question whether "scientific languages" are languages is not a serious one. To raise it is as pointless as asking whether airplanes *really* fly or cameras *really* see. There is no study of "language" ranging from ants, to chimps, to human language, to formal arithmetic, any more than there is a study of "locomotion" ranging from amoeba to eagle to science-fiction space ship; or "communication," ranging from cellular interaction to Shakespeare's sonnets to "intelligent" extraterrestials.

In passing, we might note that the same considerations hold for the much-debated question of whether machines can think, opened in the modern period in a classic 1950 paper by the British mathematician Alan Turing, in which he proposed what has since been called the "Turing test" for machine intelligence. The question has aroused lively discussion and controversy, contrary to Turing's intentions. He regarded the question as "too meaningless to deserve discussion," though in half a century, he speculated, conditions might have changed enough for us to alter our usage, just as some languages use the metaphor of flying for airplanes. Turing seems to have agreed with Wittgenstein as to the pointlessness of the discussion and debate that has ensued, until today, over whether machines can (in principle) think, play chess, understand Chinese, do long division, etc., and about how we could "empirically" establish that they do; or whether robots can reach for objects and pick them up, murder, and so on.

I think Turing's stand was correct. These are questions of decision about sharpening and altering usage, not fact, just as there is no empirical question of whether airplanes can fly to London or whether submarines really set sail but do not swim. The conclusion remains if we add further sensory conditions or criteria beyond performance, as has been proposed.

A completely separate issue is whether simulation might teach us something about the process simulated; whether a chess-playing program, for example, might teach us something about human thought. In the latter case, the topic is very badly chosen, in my opinion, but in principle simulation certainly can provide much insight. That much was well understood centuries ago, though the classical discussion did not fall into the errors of the modern revival. When Jacques de Vaucanson amazed observers with his remarkable contrivances, he and his audience were concerned to understand the animate systems he was modelling. His clockwork duck, for example, was intended to be a model of the actual digestion of a duck, not a facsimile that might fool his audience, the neuropsychologist John Marshall points out in a recent study. That is the purpose of simulation generally in the natural sciences. There is little if any role here for operational tests of one or another sort, and surely no point in a debate over whether Vaucanson's duck *really* digests. In this regard, there has been considerable regression in the modern "cognitive revolution," in my opinion, though Turing himself was clear about the matter.

Returning to the Fregean picture as a kind of frictionless plane, the first question that arises concerns language: is the picture presented in any meaningful sense an ideal to which human language might be an approximation? That has to be argued, not merely presupposed; it seems unlikely to withstand analysis. A second question concerns thinking. Does the scientific enterprise employ the same mechanisms as ordinary thought and inquiry? Over a broad spectrum in psychology, philosophy, speculative neurophysiology, artificial intelligence, and cognitive science, it has been assumed that there are "mechanisms of general intelligence," general procedures that apply indifferently to various cognitive domains. This "uniformity assumption" has deep roots. But we should take some care to sort out the components of the traditional beliefs.

At the origins of modern rationalist psychology, Lord Herbert discussed the "principles or notions implanted in the mind" that "we bring to objects from ourselves . . . as . . . a direct gift of Nature, a precept of

natural instinct"; these " common notions" and "intellectual truths" are "imprinted on the soul by the dictates of
Nature itself," and though "stimulated by objects" are not
"conveyed" by them. Similar ideas were later developed
in Cartesian psychology and by Cambridge Platonists, in
a particularly rich way, including a version of Gestalt
psychology. In Hume's terms much later, part of human
knowledge derives "from the original hand of nature" as
"a species of instinct." "The common sense of mankind,"
"Thomas Reid held, consists of "original and natural
judgments" that are "a part of that furniture which nature
hath given to the human understanding" and "direct us in
the common affairs of life." This "epistemic naturalism"
has reappeared in the modern period in several forms,
including W.V. Quine's influential "naturalized episte-
mology," which represents a sharp and unwarranted
departure from the natural sciences, in my opinion; and
in other versions, such as Strawson's suggestion that we
have a "general framework of beliefs to which we are
inescapably committed" by virtue of our nature (so that
debate with the skeptic is idle, he argues). The epistemic
naturalism of early modern thought appears to be quite
reasonable, and is being rediscovered and given more
substance in current empirical research.

A separate question is what this has to do with the
human activity called "science," which has little regard
for "the common sense of mankind," and is happy to
dismiss beliefs "to which we are inescapably committed," such as the inescapable belief that the sun is
dropping below the horizon or that space is Euclidean.
Doubtless scientific inquiry too is based on principles
"imprinted on the soul by the dictates of Nature itself,"
but it has to be shown that these are the same as those that

"direct us in the common affairs of life," as commonly assumed. That is far from obvious.

Inquiry into particular abilities, aspects of knowledge and belief, and so on, has regularly found that the various subcomponents of the mind function quite differently. Proposals as to what may be common seem to reduce to trivialities, such as "break a task into subparts"; when particular tasks are directly addressed, special structure is invariably built in. Little is known about how we handle "the common affairs of life," or those uncommon affairs called "science." Study of its history, or engagement in the craft, indicates that it is guided by curious concepts of intelligibility and insight that are very difficult to convey, but that one can sense in important work and that students somehow "learn by doing." Living one's life is a creative activity too. There is little reason to suppose it to be conducted with general skills and methods without special adaptations, or to believe that such devices apply as well to the specialized forms of creativity that humans engage in, and come to appreciate, when they move beyond the "common affairs."

In domains where understanding goes beneath the surface, we seem to find special structure and design. It's not clear why we should take seriously the possibility that in just those domains where little or nothing is understood, an otherwise unknown uniformity principle applies. It is still less clear why we should take seriously the extensive current discussion of the potential implications of unstructured alternatives to specific articulated theories, say neural net or statistical approaches to language, could they be devised; similarly, no embryologist would be much interested in the proposal that unstructured systems with unknown properties might some day account for development of organisms without appeal to intricate theories involving concentration of chemicals, the cell's internal program, production of proteins, and so on; some imaginary "connectionist" system, perhaps.

Collapse of the traditional uniformity hypothesis should not come as a surprise. We find nothing like it in the study of other complex systems: the visual cortex, the kidney, the circulatory system, and others. Each of these "organs of the body" has its properties. They fall together, presumably, at the level of cellular biology, but no "organ theory" deals with the properties of organs in general. The various faculties and cognitive systems of the mind may be much the same. If so, there will be no field of "cognitive science" dealing with the general properties of cognitive systems. Specifically, the study of language will neither provide a useful model for other parts of the study of the mind, nor draw from them significantly.

Note that, if true, this implies nothing about how language interacts with other mental faculties and systems; surely the interactions are dense and close, but that is another matter entirely.

We have, by now, fairly substantial evidence that one of the components of the mind/brain is a language faculty, dedicated to language and its use—where by "language," now, we mean human language, not various metaphoric extensions of the term. Other components provide "common sense understanding" of the world and our place in it—what is often called "folk psychology" and the like, though we should be careful to observe the practice of serious ethnoscience, distinguishing parochial and culture-bound notions from the elements of "folk theories" that are a common human endowment, "a direct gift of Nature"; not an easy problem, and one that is, I think, too lightly dismissed. Other components make it possible for humans to conduct scientific and mathematical inquiry, and sometimes to achieve remarkable insight: we may call them "the science-forming faculty," to dignify ignorance with a title. These could be quite different in character from those that yield "common sense understanding" in its various forms. It is an open empirical question, and no dogmatism is in order. The history of modern science perhaps suggests that the distinctions are not trivial; at least, that is one way to interpret the startling conflicts that have arisen between common sense understanding and what scientific inquiry reveals.

Speculating beyond the little that is known, we might take the mind/brain to be a complex system with a highly differentiated structure, with separate "faculties," such as the language faculty, those involved in moral and aesthetic judgment and in the special kind of rational inquiry undertaken in the natural sciences, and much else. The methods and goals of the scientific enterprise may tell us little about human thought in general, just as the symbolic systems constructed appear to differ radically from natural languages in their formal and semantic properties. If so, the picture that has guided the most important work on these topics in the last century may be seriously misconceived.

It is, I think, useful to deepen the historical perspective beyond the Fregean paradigm and consider the "first cognitive revolution," the Cartesian theory of body and mind. Descartes offered a sketchy account of the physical world in terms of the "mechanical philosophy"; basically, the view that things affect one another by contact. He tried to show that in these terms one can explain everything in the inorganic world, and a large part of the organic world as well, including everything about plants and animals and much of the functioning of humans, up to elements of sensation and perception.

In the course of this sketch, Descartes laid the foundations for modern neurophysiology, among other contributions. He also demolished the neoscholastic theory of perception, which assumed that the form of a perceived object implants itself in the brain in some mysterious fashion—obviously, not in accord with the mechanical philosophy. The Cartesian alternative invoked a kind of computational theory of the mind. A series of physical events, always involving only direct contact, stimulate the retina (the hand, etc.), and internal computational resources produce an image—say, of a triangle, or people walking in a crowd—on the basis of these scattered stimuli. The proposals have a contemporary flavor, and their impact was primarily in the areas that have flourished during the revival of such notions since the 1950s: vision and language.

But Descartes noticed that certain phenomena do not appear to fall within the mechanical philosophy. Specifically, he argued, no artifact could exhibit the normal properties of language use: the fact that it is unbounded in scope, not determined by external stimuli or internal state, not random but coherent and appropriate to situations though not caused by them, evoking thoughts that the hearer might have expressed the same way—a collection of properties that we may call "the creative aspect of language use." Accordingly, some new principle must be invoked; for the Cartesians, a second substance whose essence is thought. The "cognitive power is properly called mind," Descartes held, when it manifests this creative aspect, as it "forms new ideas" or "attends to those already formed," beyond the control of sense or imagination or memory.

We then have the problem of determining the nature of this *res cogitans*, and we face the unification problem that arises throughout the natural sciences: showing how mind and body interact, in the traditional formulation. The approach is basically that of the natural sciences, and the reasoning is unaffected when we move from the complex artifacts that fascinated the 17th century imagination to those that excite many of the same questions and speculations today.

We also have the problem of determining whether another object has a mind like ours. Descartes and his followers, notably Géraud de Cordemoy, outlined experimental tests that could be used to answer this question, focusing on language use. If some creature passes the hardest experiments I can devise to test whether it expresses and interprets new thoughts as I do, Cordemoy argues, it would be "unreasonable" to doubt that it has a mind like mine. Note that this is normal, garden variety science, like developing a litmus test for acidity: the task is to determine whether one of the real components of the world is present in a certain case—acidity, or a mind.

It is interesting to compare the Cartesian tests for the existence of other minds with the current reliance on the Turing test to determine "empirically" whether a machine can carry out some intelligent act (say, play chess). Again, I think it is fair to speak of a conceptual regression since the cognitive revolution of the 17th century, a change from reasonable (though incorrect) science to an approach that is foreign to the methods or concerns of the sciences.

The traditional mind/body problem is often misconceived in the recent revival. Thus Herbert Simon argues in his autobiography that a 1956 program for proving theorems of propositional calculus "solved the venerable mind/body problem, explaining how a system composed of matter can have the properties of mind" by treating symbols as material patterns. However one judges the achievement, it does not deal with the traditional mind/body problem, either the aspects just mentioned or others (say, the nature of consciousness).

As is well-known, the Cartesian program collapsed within a generation. It is commonly derided today as the belief that there is "a ghost in the machine." But that conclusion mistakes what happened. It was the Cartesian theory of body that collapsed; the theory of mind, such as it was, remained unaffected. Newton demonstrated that the Cartesian theory of the material world was fatally inadequate, unable to account for the most elementary properties of motion. He had nothing to say about the ghost in the machine; he exorcised the machine, not the ghost.

Newton found that bodies had unexpected ghostly properties; their "occult quality" of action at a distance transcends the common notion of body or material object. Like many leading scientists of the day, Newton found these results disturbing, agreeing with the Cartesians that "It is inconceivable, that inanimate brute Matter should, without the Mediation of something else, which is not material, operate upon and affect other matter without mutual Contact"; the idea of action at a distance through a vacuum is "so great an Absurdity that I believe no Man who has in philosophical matters a competent Faculty of thinking, can ever fall into it."

Newton concluded that we must accept that universal gravity exists, even if we cannot explain it in terms of the self-evident "mechanical philosophy." While "Newton seemed to draw off the veil from some of the mysteries of nature," Hume wrote in his *History of England*, "he shewed at the same time the imperfections of the mechanical philosophy; and thereby restored her ultimate secrets to that obscurity in which they ever did and ever will remain." As many commentators have observed, this intellectual move "set forth a new view of science," in which the goal is "not to seek ultimate explanations," but to find the best theoretical account we can of the phenomena of experience and experiment (I. Bernard Cohen). Conformity to common sense understanding is henceforth put aside, as a criterion for rational inquiry. If study of Newton's occult quality leads to postulation of curved space-time, so be it, however common sense may be offended thereby.

These moves also deprive us of any determinate notion of body or matter. The world is what it is, with whatever strange properties it has, including those previously called "mental." Such notions as "physicalism" or "eliminative materialism" lose any clear sense. Metaphysical dualism becomes unstateable, as does the view that "philosophical accounts of our minds, our knowledge, our language must in the end be continuous with, and harmonious with, the natural sciences" (Daniel Dennett), a view that T.R. Baldwin calls (approvingly) "metaphysical naturalism." None of these positions can be formulated coherently without a delimitation of the "material world," the domain of "the natural sciences." But what is that? Surely not what was called "physics" a century ago, or yesterday, or perhaps ever.

We seek to extend our understanding of the world and to assimilate what we find to the core natural sciences in some way, perhaps modifying them as inquiry proceeds. Ideas that yield understanding and insight are judged legitimate, part of the presumed truth about the world; our criteria of rationality and intelligibility may also change and develop, as understanding grows. If humans have "ghostly properties" apart from those common to all of matter, that's a fact about the world, which we must try to comprehend in the manner of the sciences, that is, by rational inquiry in the only way we know. Similarly, if the results of 19th century chemistry could not be accommodated by the physics of the day, it would have been an absurdity to reject the Periodic table, valence, the theory of organic molecules, and so on, on these grounds; it is no less irrational to dismiss the conclusion that the remarkable properties of form and meaning in natural language are explained by computational processes, often in quite far-reaching ways, on grounds that contemporary biology offers no apparent basis for these conclusions. As for the mind/body distinction, it cannot be formulated in anything like the Cartesian manner; or any other, as far as I can see, except as a terminological device to distinguish various aspects of the natural world.

We might turn, at this point, to a standard criticism of the Fregean paradigm for its avowed Platonism, which is held to violate the conditions of metaphysical naturalism. As Baldwin expresses the critique, Frege's "hypothesis is not 'continuous with' those advanced by the natural sciences." The reason lies in Frege's hypothesis that grasping a thought

> is a process which takes place on the very confines of the mental and which for that reason cannot be completely understood from a purely psychological standpoint. For in grasping the law something comes into view whose nature is no longer mental in the proper sense, namely the thought; and this process is perhaps the most mysterious of all.

Frege's position, Baldwin agrees, conflicts with the doctrine that "all fundamental forces are physical" by positing a *thought* that is objective but not physical, and by postulating a process of "grasping a thought" that cannot be incorporated within the natural sciences. The critique assumes that "metaphysical naturalism" is an intelligible doctrine, based upon some delimitation of the domain of "the physical" that excludes Fregean "thoughts" in principle, but includes mathematical objects that "push each other about," massless particles, curved space-time, infinite one-dimensional strings in 10-dimensional space, and whatever will be contrived tomorrow. But until the delimitation is explained, we cannot understand the critique. At least, I cannot.

Though metaphysical naturalism appears to be unformulable, we can formulate a kind of *methodological* naturalism, which holds that study of the mind is an inquiry into certain aspects of the natural world, including what have traditionally been called mental events, processes, and states, and that we should investigate these aspects of the world as we do any others, attempting to construct intelligible explanatory theories that provide insight and understanding of phenomena that are selected to advance the search into deeper principles. We do not assume a metaphysical divide when we speak of chemical events, processes and states, and the same should be true of the domain of the mental, if we borrow traditional terms for descriptive purposes. This "natural-istic approach" will look forward to eventual integration with the core natural sciences, but whether that is possible in principle, or for a human intelligence, is a question of fact, not dogma. This approach—what I will henceforth mean by "naturalism"—should be uncontentious, though its reach remains to be determined.

Plainly, such an approach does not exclude other ways of trying to comprehend the world. Someone committed to it (as I am) can consistently believe (as I do) that we learn much more of human interest about how people think and feel and act by reading novels or studying history than from all of naturalistic psychology, and perhaps always will; similarly, the arts may offer appreciation of the heavens to which astrophysics cannot aspire. We are speaking here of theoretical understanding, a particular mode of comprehension. In this domain, any departure from a naturalistic approach carries a burden of justification. Perhaps one can be given, but I know of none. Departures from this naturalistic approach are not uncommon, including, in my opinion, much of the most reflective and considered work in the philosophy of language and mind, a fact that merits some thought, if true.

A naturalistic approach will assume that like other complex systems, the human brain can be profitably viewed as an array of interacting subcomponents, which can be studied at various levels: atoms, cells, cell assemblies, neural networks, computational systems of the kind pioneered, at a primitive stage, by the Cartesians, and so on. We cannot know in advance which (if any) of these approaches will provide insight and understanding. In several domains, including language, the computational approaches currently have the strongest claim to scientific status, at least on naturalistic grounds.

We might ask whether a study of the brain in such terms is improper or controversial. If not, we then ask whether the theories developed are true. Does the brain in fact have the architecture, subsystems, states, properties, spelled out in some particular theory? As for the first query, it is hardly controversial to suppose that the brain, like other complex systems, has subsystems with states and properties. The properties attributed in computational theories are by and large well understood. No general conceptual issues seem to arise, only questions of truth, the second query, which we may put aside here.

It has been common to try to relieve uneasiness about computational approaches by invoking computer models to show that we have robust, hard-headed instances of the kind: psychology then studies software problems. That is a dubious move. Artifacts pose all kinds of questions that do not arise in the case of natural objects. Whether some object is a key or a table or a computer depends on designer's intent, standard use, mode of interpretation, and so on. The same considerations arise when we ask whether the device is malfunctioning, following a rule, etc. There is no natural kind or normal case. The hardware-software distinction is a matter of interpretation, not simply of physical structure, though with further assumptions about intention, design, and use we could sharpen it. Such questions do not arise in the study of organic molecules, nematodes, the language faculty, or other natural objects, viewed (to the extent we can achieve this standpoint) as what they are, not in a highly intricate and shifting space of human interests and concerns. The belief that there was a problem to resolve, beyond the normal ones, reflects an unwarranted departure from naturalism; the solution offered carries us from a manageable frying pan to a fire that is out of control.

We naturally want to solve the unification problem, that is, to relate studies of the brain undertaken at various levels. Sometimes unification will be reductive, as when much of biology was incorporated within known biochemistry; sometimes it may require radical modification of the more "fundamental" discipline, as when physics was "expanded" in the new quantum theory, enabling it to account for properties that had been discovered and explained by chemists. We cannot know in advance what course unification will take, if it succeeds at all.

If there are answers to the questions we raise, there is no guarantee that we can find them; or that we are capable of asking the right questions in the first place. Any organism has certain ways of perceiving and interpreting the world, a certain "Umwelt" or "cognitive space," determined in large part by its specific nature and by general properties of biological systems. Given an organism with its special cognitive systems, we can identify a category of "problem situations" in which it might find itself: an array of circumstances that it perceives and interprets in a certain way by virtue of its nature and prior history, including (for humans) questions that are posed and background belief and understanding that are brought to bear on them, and even problem situations that are contrived on the basis of theory-driven considerations and approached with a degree of self-awareness—the activity that we call "science." Some problem situations fall within the animal's cognitive capacities, others not. Let us call these "problems" and "mysteries," respectively. The concepts are relative to an organism: what is a mystery for a rat might be only a problem for a monkey, and conversely. For a rat, a "prime number maze" (turn right at every prime choice point), or even far simpler ones, is a permanent mystery; the rat does not have the cognitive resources to deal with it, though a human might. A radial maze, in contrast, poses a problem that a rat might solve quite well. The distinctions need not be absolute, but they can hardly fail to be real.

If humans are part of the natural world, not angels, the same is true of them: there are problems that we might hope to solve, and mysteries that will be forever beyond our cognitive reach. As reflective beings, we may well seek solutions to mysteries, always failing. There might even arise a discipline dedicated to this quest, separating from the natural sciences as they become increasingly self-conscious and focused on problems. In forthcoming work, Colin McGinn suggests that there indeed is such a discipline: philosophy, deliberating about questions that appear to be of peculiar depth and "hardness," being mysteries-for-humans. Philosophical questions would then be the "formulable mysteries" (for humans).

We might think of the natural sciences as a kind of chance convergence between aspects of the natural world and properties of the human mind/brain, which has allowed some rays of light to penetrate the general obscurity; *chance* convergence, in that nothing in nature has "designed" us to deal with quandaries we face and can sometimes formulate. Since Charles Sanders Peirce, there have been proposals about evolutionary factors that allegedly guarantee that we can find the truth about the world, and there are much earlier beliefs about our unique access to the nature of our own minds and their products. But such speculations seem groundless. We should not, I think, too quickly dismiss Descartes's speculation that we may not "have intelligence enough" to comprehend the creative aspect of language use and other kinds of free choice and action, though "we are so conscious of the liberty and indifference which exists in us that there is nothing that we comprehend more clearly and perfectly," and "it would be absurd to doubt that of which we inwardly experience and perceive as existing within ourselves" just because it lies beyond our comprehension. That could be true, consistent with anything we know about the natural world. If central domains of the "mental" are cognitively inaccessible to us, we shall have to learn about humans, as best we can, in some way other than naturalistic inquiry.

Returning to Newton's demolition of the common sense theory of body, the natural conclusion is that human thought and action are properties of organized matter, like "powers of attraction and repulsion," electrical charge, and so on. That conclusion was drawn very soon, most forcefully by La Mettrie, a generation later by the eminent chemist Joseph Priestley, though neither attempted to deal with the properties of mind identified by the Cartesians, just as they have been put aside in the revival of "cognitive science" since the 1950s.

Drawing the natural conclusion, we face a series of questions: What exactly are these properties of things in the world? How do they arise in the individual and the species? How are they put to use in action and interpretation? How can organized matter have these properties (the new version of the unification problem)?

Certain aspects of these questions have been productively investigated. In the case of language, it has been possible to study a number of traditional questions that had eluded serious inquiry, and more recently, to recast them significantly, leading to much new understanding of at least some central features of the mind and its functioning. The fundamental Cartesian questions remain elusive, however; matter and mind are not two categories of things, but they appear to pose entirely different kinds of quandaries for human intelligence.

Pursuing a naturalistic course as far as it reaches, we turn to the investigation of particular faculties of the mind. As Descartes concluded, the language faculty is, to a good approximation, a common human attribute, and apparently unique to the species in essential respects; at least, nothing remotely similar has been detected elsewhere in the biological world. Its "initial state" is determined by genetic endowment. Under the triggering and (marginally) shaping effect of experience, it passes through a series of states and attains a relatively stable "steady state" at about puberty, changing later only in peripheral respects. In each state, we may distinguish two components: a cognitive system and performance systems. The cognitive system stores information that is accessed by the performance systems, which use it for articulation, interpretation, expression of thought, asking questions, referring, and so on. The cognitive system accounts for our infinite knowledge; for example, our knowledge about sound and meaning and their relations over an unbounded range. There is by now a large mass of reliable data about these matters from a variety of typologically different languages, and nontrivial theories that go some distance in explaining the evidence.

The performance systems are generally assumed to be

fixed and invariant. The reason is, basically, ignorance. There is no evidence that this simplest assumption is false. The cognitive systems, however, do vary: my language is not that of a person in East Africa—or, for that matter, that of my brother, wife, or children, and surely not that of my parents. The variety cannot be great, of that we can be sure; external conditions are far too impoverished to have more than a marginal impact on the highly articulated and intricate structures that arise as the language faculty develops in its normal course. We could not have acquired any language unless its fundamental properties were already in place, in advance of experience, as argued in the epistemic naturalism of early rationalist psychology. The scientific problem is to establish explicitly what we assume must be true, as in studying embryology, the onset of puberty, and other aspects of growth and development. By now, enough is known to indicate that the differences among languages may not be very impressive compared with the overwhelming commonality, at least from the standpoint we adopt towards organisms other than ourselves.

It is by virtue of the way the cognitive system is embedded in performance systems that the formal properties of expressions are interpreted as rhyme, entailment, and so on. The information provided by lexical items and other expressions yields perspectives for thinking and speaking about the world by virtue of the way their elements are interpreted "at the interface"; embedded in different performance systems in some hypothetical (perhaps biologically impossible) organism, they could serve as instructions for some other activity, say locomotion. We are studying a real object, the language faculty of the brain, which has assumed a particular state that provides instructions to performance systems that play a role in articulation, interpretation, expression of beliefs and desires, referring, telling stories, and so on. For such reasons, the topic is human language.

We may say that Peter has (knows, speaks, . . .) the language L when the cognitive component of Peter's language faculty is in the state L. So regarded, the language is a way to speak and understand, a traditional conception. The cognitive system is a generative procedure that determines an infinite class of linguistic expressions, each a collection of instructions for the performance systems. Particular signs, in the Fregean sense, are manifestations of linguistic expressions (spoken, written, signed, whatever); speech acts are manifestations of linguistic expressions in a broader sense.

Pursuing this course, we can progress towards understanding of some aspects of the Cartesian problem: the "infinite use of finite means," as Wilhelm von Humboldt rephrased it. The tradition persisted through the 19th century and beyond, increasingly diverging from what was considered "scientific linguistics." As modern behavioral science and structuralist approaches were taking form 70 years ago, the Danish linguist Otto Jespersen recognized that the central concern of the linguist must be free creation, the ability of each person to construct and understand "free expressions," typically new, each a sound with a meaning. More deeply, the task is to discover how the structures that underlie this ability "come into existence in the mind of a speaker" who, "without any grammatical instruction, from innumerable sentences heard and understood . . . will abstract some notion of their structure which is definite enough to guide him in framing sentences of his own." Though important and basically correct, these ideas had little impact, unlike the far narrower Saussurean conceptions and behaviorist doctrines, which were enormously influential.

The traditional ideas could not receive clear expression until the formal sciences provided the concept of generative (recursive) procedure. The modern study of these questions might be regarded as a confluence of traditional ideas that had been dismissed as senseless or unworkable, with new formal insights that made it possible to pursue them seriously.

Work of the past few years has to some extent succeeded in identifying general principles of language that can be attributed to initial endowment, with options of variation restricted to subparts of the lexicon. The "computational system" of language that determines the forms and relations of linguistic expressions may indeed be invariant; in this sense, there is only one human language, as a rational Martian observing humans would have assumed. Acquisition of a particular language is the process of fixing the lexical options on the basis of simple and accessible data. One goal of research, now at least formulable in a realistic way, is to be able literally to deduce Hungarian or Swahili by fixing the options within the finite lexical variety allowed.

The picture that is emerging is the first really significant departure from a rich tradition extending to Indian grammar 2500 years ago, later Greek grammar and its descendants, which always took a language to be a system of rules that are specific to particular constructions in that language: rules for forming questions in English, for example. The reopening of the traditional questions 40 years ago kept these assumptions intact. But mistakenly, it now seems. Grammatical constructions such as relative clause, passive, verbal phrase, and so on, appear to be taxonomic artifacts, like "terrestial mammal" or "household pet"; the array of phenomena derive from the interaction of principles of much greater generality. Still more recent work indicates that these principles may themselves be epiphenomenal, their consequences reducing to more general and abstract properties of the computational system, properties that have a kind of "least effort" flavor. This "minimalist" program also seeks to reduce the descriptive technology to the level of virtual conceptual necessity, sharply restricting the devices available for description, which means that the complex phenomena of widely varied languages must be explained in terms of abstract principles of economy of derivation and representation. An expression of the language L, then, would be a formal object that satisfies the universal interface conditions in the optimal way, given the lexical options for L. Such a program faces an extremely heavy empirical burden. If these directions prove correct, they should yield much deeper insight into the computational processes that underlie our linguistic abilities, processes that seem radically different from what was assumed only a few years ago.

This conception of language critically introduces global properties of computations of a kind that are known to yield extreme computational complexity; it predicts that language should be unusable, to a considerable degree. The general conclusion is surely correct. It is well known that language is "badly adapted to use"; of the class of "free expressions" determined by the "notion of structure" in our minds, only scattered fragments are readily usable. Even short and simple expressions often cannot be handled easily by our performance systems; the same is true of simple problems of reasoning, a fact that in itself may tell us little about our reasoning capacities. Furthermore, usability cross-cuts deviance; some deviant expressions are perfectly comprehensible, while non-deviant ones often are processed inaccurately (with respect to the cognitive system). The unusability of language does not interfere with communication: speaker and hearer have similar languages and (perhaps identical) performance systems, so what one can produce, the other can interpret, over a large range.

It remains to be shown, however, that the specific predictions about usability are correct. That is a hard and interesting problem, just coming into focus, standing alongside the older problem of explaining a broad range of properties of sound and meaning, many only recently discovered, and approaching the unification problem—in brief, showing how the brain, which appears superficially to be so "messy," can produce something with the curious digital and computational properties of form and meaning in natural language.

It is the *mechanisms* that enter into thought and action that have proven most amenable to inquiry. In the study of language, there is new understanding of the computational systems of the mind/brain, including those commonly called "phonetic" or "semantic," though in fact, all are "syntactic" in the broader sense that they have to do with mental representations. A good deal is known about the acquisition of these systems, and about how perceptual-articulatory systems interpret and use the instructions they provide; there are also many interesting ideas about the "conceptual-intentional" interface, a harder but not completely recalcitrant problem. The limits of the 17th century revolution have not, however, been transcended. The fundamental Cartesian issues still lie far beyond reach: the creative aspect of language use, and more generally, the nature of actions that are appropriate, coherent, and intelligible but apparently uncaused, those we may be "incited and inclined" to perform, though not "compelled," and the properties of free creation that are "properly called mind."

All of these topics—including the ones that seem to be mysteries—still fall within the lower form of human intelligence, to borrow the terms of the Spanish philosopher-physician Juan Huarte in the late 16th century. They arise in connection with the "generative faculty" of ordinary understanding, which is foreign to "beasts and plants" but falls short of true exercise of the creative imagination, something that may involve "a mixture of madness." Even the lower form lies beyond the reach of our theoretical understanding, apart from the study of the mechanism that constitute it, at least for now, perhaps forever. We should not necessarily regard that as an unhappy outcome, in my opinion.

Noam Chomsky

DISCUSSION

DISCUSSION

Dr. Eric Wanner (Moderator): I want to thank Noam Chomsky very much and proceed to the discussion. It is perhaps a symptom of what I probably should call the cognitive sciences—and not cognitive science—that we have as our panel a philosopher, a psychologist, and a neuroscientist. It is also surely a symptom of the range and impact of Noam Chomsky's ideas. For alphabetical reasons only, we will begin with philosophy, and it turns out accidentally, proceed in decreasing levels of abstraction through psychology and neuroscience. Our first discussant is Professor Akeel Bilgrami of Columbia University.

Professor Akeel Bilgrami: Chomsky's paper has a complicated dialectic which is complicated in many ways. On the one hand it questions a number of philosophical assumptions that frame a certain picture of language and thought, which he calls the Fregean picture. On the other hand it rejects various questions (such as the question:

can machines think?) which philosophers, and cognitive scientists have asked as not being well-formed questions and therefore leading to no particular worthy intellectual pursuit. It also finds certain attitudes that philosophers strike (such as for instance what he calls 'metaphysical naturalism') to be dogmatic and in some sense even inconsistent. At the end of all this accumulated critique, he offers some positive suggestions both methodological and theoretically substantive on his chosen theme of language and thought. And in the midst of all this complex and detailed business he slips in a rather beautiful historical diagnosis of what was right and what wrong in the Cartesian philosophy, a diagnosis which turns on its head this century's fashion for treating Descartes as a philosophical leper; and it is worth pointing out that he manages to do this without the slightest concession to recent rearguard, subjectivist Cartesian tendencies in such philosophers as John Searle and Tom Nagel.

My brief comments on a paper of such rich perspective and panoramic scope will of necessity have to be highly selective.

Those in the audience who are not directly involved in Chomsky's areas of interest will perhaps take the fierce seriousness and detail with which his arguments are mounted and his proposals offered as betraying a technical and narrow conception of his subject. This is a natural conflation for those unfamiliar with the developments in this disciplines. But though it might be natural, the conflation is thoroughly unfair and misses the point of one of his most central claims. Indeed I think it is fair to say that from the inside of these disciplines, in particular the discipline of the Philosophy of Language, it is Chomsky's position rather than many of the other current views that he is criticizing, which liberates the subject from artificial, distorting and narrowing theories about the nature of meaning and the content of thought. Let me explain.

Lets begin with the criticisms in his paper of the social conception of language as well as of the related idea that there is something essentially and intrinsically normative in the study of meaning. According to this assumption if someone living and speaking, say, in this upper-East side community were to say out of medical ignorance, "I have arthritis in my thigh" he would be saying something false. This is because in this community the meaning of 'arthritis' is that it is a disease of the joints only. On Chomsky's view however no clear sense can be made of the idea of what meaning is in a community and so no sense can be made of the idea that on an individual's lips the meaning of 'arthritis' or of any other term is constituted by communal usage. Therefore on his view there is no particular compulsion to think of that utterance as false. It should be just as possible to say that that individual's term 'arthritis' means a wider class of ailment which afflicts both joints and ligaments. If so his utterance "I have arthritis in my thigh", given *his* meaning of arthritis, is a true utterance. This denial of social or communal determinations of meaning is closely linked with his denial of a certain kind of normativity of meaning. What fills philosophers with qualm is that, if Chomsky is right, there will be no scope to assess our protagonist as saying something false or as making a mistake: we can at best say that his individual language does not coincide in this lexical fragment with his neighbour's, say, a practising M.D. This compulsion to find speakers correct or mistaken in this respect flows precisely from a commitment to the normativity of meaning which is missing in Chomsky's view. Chomsky points out that there is nothing of theoretical interest in the idea of such norms of language because such norms are not intrinsic to the idea of meaning, they have more to do with authority structures that lie outside of the notion of language, and it merely paralyses the prospect of giving an account of language and the cognitive aspects underlying our mastery of it, to go beyond individual languages to a pretence of a more social and norm-governed phenomenon. The point is part of a soberly made critique based on a realistic sense of what of what is theoretically tractable and identifiable. This has given the impression to many that he is narrowing the subject to leave out interesting social and normative elements. Exactly the opposite is true for he has liberated the study of language from a set of unnecessary and ill-described constraints. And my suspicion is that the impression is largely a matter of being misled by the presentation. If Chomsky had made his point more flamboyantly and with the requisite hyperbole, as say Foucault might have, and said that the philosopher's hankering to assess usage for a certain kind of correctness and mistakenness, and therefore his elevation of the authority figure in the community (in this case, the doctor) as having some intrinsic normative relevance for meaning, was just a sublimated form of the 'will to power', then I suspect he would be applauded for having liberated the study of language in precisely the way he has.

There is another point on which there is much uncomprehending complaint. The *non-specialist* is often heard to say that Chomsky is too scientistic about his subject of language and thought and ignores the fact that language is a subtle craft, a mysterious art and a cultural instrument of great power. But again the plain fact is that Chomsky is more clear-headed than most other theorists and philosophers of language about how much of language as commonly conceived is *not* susceptible to scientific inquiry; and it is only because he has seen through the trumped up notions of language which are the object of other more theoretically ambitious philosophical accounts that he can afford to be clearer than others about this. Evidence of this may be found in the fact that exactly *the opposite* complaint is made by the *specialists*, who have consistently said that he has unnecessarily restricted scientific and formal theorizing to certain aspects of syntax and formal semantics leaving the lexical aspect of semantics ("meaning") out in the cold. Let me explain again.

As he points out in his paper, one of the crucial points in his overall conception of language is that the lexical aspects of language are to be thought of as bringing in an agent's *perspective* on things in the world. This is in marked contrast to those philosophers who treat the items in the lexicon in terms of the concept of *reference* to things in the world. This difference makes all the difference to what is at present scientifically tractable and what is not. If one thought that the names and predicates in our language were best studied as referring to objects or classes of objects in the world, then there would be a temptation to think that meaning and semantics could be naturalized. That is to say, the idea that the word 'cow', for instance, refers to cows could be seen as constructible from and therefore reducible to the idea that individual occurrences of the representation 'cow' in an individual psychological economy stand in a regular (though of course not exceptionless) causal relations with actual cows. Since these are purely causal facts we can see meaning, conceived referentially along these lines, as strictly subsumable under scientific laws. That is we can have laws covering everybody who has representations of this kind because more or less everybody stands in causal relations to more or less the same things in the world around them. We can thus make semantics and intentional psychology a scientific enterprise with universal generalizations.

Though I have obviously had to put it very crudely in the time I have, I don't think I have done any violence whatsoever to Jerry Fodor's view of things in the exposition of this last paragraph.

Now it is precisely this conception of meaning that Chomsky has resisted when he rejects the idea of reference to things in the study of the lexicon and speaks instead of a linguistic agent's perspective on things. Perspectives unlike reference are messy things. As far as meaning is concerned, they introduce such things as beliefs as mediating the things in the world with which we stand in causal relations, and in particular they introduce an element that is too various and too shifting between one context of representation and another. A chemically knowledgeable person's representation of 'water' no doubt stands in causal relations to water just as the chemical ignoramus's, but their perspectives on the same substance are naturally entirely different because one has chemical beliefs that the other does not. So the universal laws covering all those who have these representations are simply not to be had. If there are to be any generalizations, if we are ever to say that these two people have the same meanings or concepts which explain their linguistic and other behaviour it can only be in particular contexts or localities where the chemical beliefs and knowledge of the one are not relevant. To say that generalizations are highly localized in this way is precisely to say what Chomsky says in his lecture: that we should leave certain aspects of language and thought to the illumination that non-scientific enterprises such as commonsense psychology and history and literature attempt to shed. The point is that the claim to science in this field was only possible while one worked with a trumped up externalist, referentialist picture of language as object of study. Thus the *non-specialist's* impression of technical narrowness in Chomsky is unfair in just the proportion that the *specialist's* complaint and aspirations are misplaced.

Here let me add a few remarks to Chomsky's own by way of diagnosis. A good question to ask is: why does the effort to see meaning in terms of reference and external causality seem too high a cost to pay for making the subject naturalistically and scientifically tractable? The short answer of course is because it leaves the perspectival element out. But the question really is: what underlies the stress on perspective that Chomsky takes to be essential to the lexicon. The answer has, I think, to do with self-knowledge. And it can be given with the help of a contrast within Chomsky's own overall picture. Those aspects of formal semantics and of syntax that Chomsky places within the ken of universal grammar and that fall easily within methodological naturalism's scientific efforts are indeed aspects of our cognitive make-up. That is, the theory of grammar here captures things we know (or 'cognize' as Chomsky puts it somewhere). But the lexical aspect brings in an element for which something more than this may seem intuitively to be in play. My term 'arthritis' or 'cow' or 'London' are caught up with certain perspectives on things in the world, and these are of course nothing over and above my conceptions and beliefs. But I think unlike the knowledge or cognizings attributed by the other aspects of the theory of syntax, there is an intuition that even when the perspective or conceptions involved in my concept of, say, London are not on the forefront of my mind, I could, with enough attention and recall, bring them with more or less success to the forefront of my mind, even if I can't always verbalize them. But no such requirement of self-knowledge is intuitively felt for the knowledge and beliefs attributed by the theory of the non-lexical and formal aspects of semantics or by the theory of syntax. There, recall and attention are not likely to bring anything substantial or precise to the forefront of our own minds. Only something like an education in the linguistics department at the Massachusetts Institute of Technology will bring that about. If this is right, that is if it is right that only the perspectival element that Chomsky stresses in the lexicon consists of knowledge or cognizings or beliefs that are themselves known to the agent in this way, then we are in a position to see why purely referential and external causal relations will not capture what is essential to the lexical aspect of language.

So for example, chemically ignorant as well as chemically knowledgeable agents stand in causal relations with H_2O, but it would be quite wrong to form universal generalizations and attribute to the former (the ignorant) the same concept of water in all contexts as one would attribute it to the latter (the knowledgeable). The reason is that to do so is to attribute to the former beliefs and intentional states that they could not possibly have self-knowledge of through recall and attention. So the diagnosis I am offering for why these efforts at scientific treatment of lexical meaning are bound to fail at present is based on an intuitively held principle, and I should be curious to know what Chomsky would say in response to it. The principle is just this. Unlike syntax and the non-lexical and formal aspects of semantics, when the subject is the lexicon and its perspectival element, self-knowledge of this kind is taken for granted unless there are *psychological* obstacles to it, such as self-deception or inattention etc. What we will not allow, according to this principle, is precisely what many philosophers have uncritically taken for granted: that self-knowledge of our perspectives, beliefs and conceptions can be threatened by obstacles that come from non-psychological sources such as those posited by abstract philosophical theories of reference.

This principle fits in nicely, I think, with Chomsky's resistance in his paper to the notion, owing to Frege, that when we attribute a thought to someone we are attributing some object to which he is related by his thinking it. If there were such 'objects of thought' it would be possible for someone to say that I could fail to know my own thoughts because I could fail to know a lot of things about these objects of thought, just as I might fail to know many things about other sorts of objects, non-mental objects such as cows or water or London. It is because we can fail to know many things about water that the chemically ignorant and the chemically knowledgeable have different perspectives on these things and their respective terms for water, despite orthographic coincidence, must be individually treated. But the *perspectives themselves* are not objects like London and water to which we are epistemologically related as Frege claimed, and that is why we cannot be ignorant about these perspectives, we cannot fail to have self-knowledge of them except of course if there are purely internal psychological censors such as self-deception etc.

All this I say by way of diagnosing what may underlie and underpin Chomsky's doubts about the scientific aspirations for the more common-sense aspects of language that come with the lexicon, and if I'm right these doubts can now be integrated with what at first sight seem altogether independent doubts about the idea of Fregean objects of thought. Both the idea that lexical meaning involves an external causal and naturalistically and scientifically tractable notion of reference, as well as the idea of objects of thought, undermine the principle that one's own perspectives on the world are, barring internal psychological censors and obstacles, transparent to one.

None of this is to suggest that we may not one day have a theory of perspectives which would describe perspectives in a way that we would not as agents have self-knowledge of them, under those descriptions. But even so, my point is that when we do such a theory, what we would have if we got it is a theory of something that would also have descriptions under which we would have self-knowledge of them, unless there were psychological obstacles of the sort I mentioned.

Let me conclude by changing the subject to the Turing test for intelligence and thought, and raise a final question for Chomsky. Chomsky's view on contemporary uses of such tests is that they are based on an ill-conceived question: Can machines think? But I wonder if there is

not a somewhat different and perfectly good question that
they can be used to raise, a question to which his own
conception of language provides a decisively negative
answer, thereby proving (as Popper might have said) that
the question was a sharp and well-formed one. This is the
question whether the idea of intelligence and thought is
something that is exhaustively characterizable in behav-
ioural and, generally, external terms that leave out anything internal to the agent. Here's what I have in mind.
Imagine a machine that produces all the verbal responses
any one of us does to all the things it hears and sees and
encounters, which we may imagine is identical to what
any one of us encounters. The only difference is that all
its responses are canned; unlike us it is not a generative
creature but is instead following a very long list of
elaborate, counterfactually formulated instructions. The
idea of such a list is not inconceivable of course since it
is a finite list. This is because its responses which
perfectly mimics one of us are going to be finite since we
ourselves are creatures with finite lives. Now if generativity is basic to language and intelligence and thought, as
Chomsky has himself always insisted, that is proof that
the machine which *ex hypothesi* passes the Turing test,
nevertheless has no more intelligence than my toaster. I
suppose some would be tempted to say that all this shows
is that for all we know *we* are not generative but merely
following a long but finite list, but that seems to be a
frivolous conclusion. And in saying it is frivolous one is
agreeing with Chomsky about the importance of generativity. What this imagined example shows rather is that
merely looking to external things like behaviour in response to the world around us is not sufficient for the
identification of thought and intelligence; we have also to

look theoretically at what is inside, at internal mechanisms and the internal cognitive and functional architecture. For example, we may test for generativity versus canned list-following in a machine by seeing what is needed to be done to a machine's functional makeup to revive it when it comes to a halt. For a generative machine we might find we could revive it by adding to its memory-space, for a non-generative machine however we would have to add to its list of instructions. And so on. The general point is that if, given Chomsky's insistence on the criterion of generativity, only tests upon *internal* mechanisms of this kind will be sufficient to answer the question about thought and intelligence, then the Turing test which makes only *external* demands is decisively refuted as a test for these things. And so my question is: doesn't this show that Turing at least in one sense helps to pose a fairly sharp question and test?

Dr. Eric Wanner: Professor Chomsky has agreed to withhold his response until all three discussants have finished. Our second discussant is Professor George Miller of Princeton University.

Professor George Miller: Thank you, Eric. I'm a very lucky person because I've been able to listen to Noam Chomsky for almost forty years now. It's always a rewarding experience. This talk today was a typically rich pattern of themes woven together in a typical graceful way. I worry about picking up any one of them lest the pattern fall apart, but there were a couple that particularly caught my attention and interested me. One was his feeling that cognitive science is headed in the wrong direction, which he expressed, implicitly at least, at several times. The other is his warning that the human intelligence may not be adequate to answer all the questions that we have been asking.

About the first one, forty years ago—almost forty years ago—for about a decade, I interacted with Noam Chomsky and with Jerry Bruner in Cambridge. The activities that we undertook jointly and separately have since been called by other people a cognitive revolution. I don't think any of us called it a cognitive revolution. We were just trying to make sense out of the obvious facts that we found in front of us, a sort of anticipation of a view that I think Noam is now calling methodological naturalism, to which I would like to subscribe in so far as I understand it.

The interesting thing to me is that within the past four or five years, all three of us, Chomsky, Bruner, and I, have publicly announced that this thing we started that has been called the cognitive revolution has been kidnapped and taken off in some direction that we disapprove of. It would be a fascinating thing for me to get the three of us together and find out whether we think the kidnappers have all done the same wrong thing. It may be that the only thing that united us forty years ago was our opposition to behaviorism, logical positivism, and a narrow structuralism in linguistics and anthropology. I don't know.

At any rate, the interesting thing to me is what Chomsky is trying to tell us would be the right direction to go. There are many, many suggestions in this rich and stimulating talk that need to be picked up and looked at carefully by psychologists, linguists, and cognitive scientists generally.

One that appeals to me is this warning that we may not

have sufficient mental capacity to achieve a reductionistic account of the mind, in which case, we'll have to settle for what we can achieve. Years ago, I heard Noam talk about the psychologist looking at the rat, and the rat, of course, is trying to solve the maze. And it's able to do that, but there are a lot of problems that the psychologist can solve that the rat doesn't even know about. I summarize this as the principle that you can't conceive of what you can't conceive of. It's been very helpful to me over the years to keep that firmly in mind.

For example, I believe that the federal government has, on the advice of some very distinguished scientists, appropriated funds for listening for intelligent life from outer space. The argument for doing this is that if we could contact a civilization, it would probably be far advanced over ours. We are just barely out of the trees, but they may be fairly far along, and think of what all the wonderful things are that we could learn by interacting with such an advanced civilization. At that point I remembered the psychologist looking at the rat. How long have we inhabited this world with rats, without the rats learning very much at all from this superior intelligence that we have. I once tried to get into an argument with Carl Sagan about this. Why is he so sure that they will not regard us as sort of a bipedal rat and try to exterminate us as we do the rat? Sagan never answered.

I do very much like the distinction between the problems that we can, perhaps eventually, solve and the mysteries that we can never solve. The problem, of course, that I have with this is telling which is which. Then, even if I knew which were the mysteries that I might set aside, I have to distinguish between which are the mysteries that I can safely accept, mysteries like action at a distance, or human consciousness, and which are the one that I should be free to doubt, like God's will, perhaps. But Chomsky didn't promise to answer all of my questions. I think he was really trying to point in the direction that a sensible cognitive scientist should try to go, and I am grateful to him for that. Thank you.

Dr. Eric Wanner: Our third discussant is Professor James Schwartz of Columbia University.

Professor James H. Schwartz: The 1960s saw two scientific revolutions important to the study of the mind/brain: the cognitive revolution that we have been talking about and the reductionist revolution of cell- and molecular biology. Both of these new approaches to understanding the mind have been extremely productive. In *my* revolution—and, despite what Mr. Ryskamp says, I am not a philosopher, nor am I a linguist—my revolution is cell- and molecular biology. I need only cite a few of the familiar advances made: an almost complete description of the molecules that mediate the conduction of the nerve impulse and of synaptic transmission, and the characterization of neurotransmitters and neuromodulators thought to be involved in pain, memory, and learning, the emotion, and the five senses. In addition, molecular and electrophysiological probes have confirmed and extended knowledge about brain areas that are critical to specific and mental functions. Thus, for example, distinct cortical regions have been identified that are specific for perceiving shape, movement, and color. Perhaps more pertinently, similar mapping of brain areas involving language is an extremely active endeavor in contemporary neuroscience.

Professor Chomsky also clearly considers *his* revolution—though he may deny it tonight—to be successful. As he recently wrote: "There is real grounds for considerable optimism about the prospects that lie ahead, not only for the study of language proper, but also for the study of cognitive systems of the mind/brain, of which language is a fundamental and essential component in the human species." It is probably not necessary to say that Professor Chomsky is justly pleased with the cognitive revolution, since he was one of the leaders of that revolution.

But as my grandmother used to say, "If we're so smart, why aren't we rich?" If the state of information on the mind/brain is so rosy, why don't we have an answer to this fundamental question: "What does the "/" mean in Chomsky's succinct formulation, mind/brain. Many of my colleagues are deeply pessimistic about the concept of mind. At their politest, they say that the gap between molecules and mind is so vast that it is absolutely fruitless to think about bridging the gap. At their worst, my colleagues warn me to stick to molecules, because it is the only hard-nosed approach. They solve the problem denying it, echoing the currently popular school of philosophy called Eliminative Materialism. This school claims that mentalist explanations of psychology, (folk psychology like my grandmother's, ultimately must reduce to neuroscience anyhow.)

So what is all of this intellectual discomfort about? In order to understand the nature of the current discomfort in the neurosciences, I believe that is necessary to review its roots. Unlike most textbook histories of science, which are told backwards from the vantage point of "the truth" of our present understanding through the hazy fog of prior error, the story should be told in the context of the history of ideas. For this purpose, it is convenient, I think, to start around 1800 with the word of Franz Joseph Gall and trace the dialectical opinions about whether mental function is discretely localized, on the one hand, or some ensemble property of the brain, on the other. Gall is still often thought of as a charlatan, along with other fashionable but obvious quacks of the late 18th century, like Count Cagliostro and Franz Anton Mesmer, because his work led to the popular pseudoscience of Phrenology. Nonetheless, if Darwin, Marx, and Freud can be considered the fathers of 20th-century thought and culture, a reasonable case can be made for Gall as grandfather of the 20th century. Why?

First, because Gall finally convinced most members of society that the brain *is* the organ of the mind. He also proposed that mental functions, both simple and complex, are situated discretely over the cerebral context. Thus, he asserted that the cortex is composed of specialized organs, each dedicated to a given mental faculty.

The conviction that the mind is situated in the brain and that mental functions are localized was extremely controversial. Inevitably, these ideas led to a materialistic view of mind that was as uncongenial to 19th-century thought as were the theories of Darwin, Marx, and Freud. Their theories forced most members of society to recognize three *other* apparently inescapable facts of life: Darwin, our biological place in nature; Marx, the fundamental importance of economic structure; and Freud, the irrational components of behavior.

There is no doubt today that the brain *is* the organ of the mind. As for Gall's other idea, on balance, the evidence accumulated so far favors the localizationists. This evidence includes the wealth of localization data from the so-called natural experiments observed by the great 19th-century neurologists. This clinical evidence for functional localization is extended by the more modern studies of neurosurgeons who have tested function removing before parts of the cortex for intractable epilepsy or tumors. In addition, the work of experimental physiologists, from David Ferrier's experiments at the end of the 19th century to experimental studies of the present day continue to provide convincing proof for localization of function. Finally, the modern techniques of brain imaging, such as positron emission tomography or PET, and magnetic resonance imaging or MRI, continue to support localization. But the key question remains: How do you get a mental event from the brain? How do discrete "organs of the mind" work? What is the meaning of the "/" in "mind/brain"?

As a matter of fact, another important aspect of Gall's influence bears directly on these questions. Gall was a psychologist. Even though an excellent neuro-anatomist, Gall developed his ideas in the long tradition of observation that could be traced to Aristotle. In the study of personality and behavior, this tradition is exemplified by physiognomy and by the description of character types. It was through observation of schoolmates with extreme character traits, and examination of the cranial features of statesmen and criminals, that Gall decided where the specific cortical organs should be. He used non-experimental—what today would be called noninvasive—techniques.

Gall was explicitly opposed to interfering with nature experimentally. In this regard, he reflected the romantic view expressed by William Wordsworth in his famous dictum, "We murder to dissect." And: "Enough of science and of art; / Close up these barren leaves. / Come forth, and hurry with your heart / That watches and receives."

It is only a slight exaggeration to think that experimental neurophysiology, from Pierre Flourens's in the 1820s to Farrier's was developed to disprove Gall's psychology. Charles Sherrington, in his 1928 obituary notice for Farrier in the Royal Society, said that Farrier proved the concept of cerebral localization and provided the basis for a "scientific phrenology."

Nonetheless, there is a sharp dissonance in approach to mind/brain between Gall, who represents the tradition of psychology, and Farrier who championed experimental neurophysiology. In a very real sense, the scientific discomfort that we are now feeling has its roots in this dialectic. Psychology analyzes brain function as related to character, personality, and social interaction, but has not yet needed any direct physiological information. In contrast, experimental neurophysiology analyzes decomposed parts of the brain, sacrificing the broad significance of function to a detailed description of physiological mechanisms. It has not yet needed any direct psychological knowledge.

To the modern reductionist mind, psychology is often thought of as a soft science, but it is curious that none of the acknowledged intellectual fathers of the 20th century —surely to be regarded as the age of technology—were experimentalists. For example, Darwin's *expression of emotions in man and animals* (1872) and most of his other work, all of Marx' writings, and all of Freud's work after his paper on hysteria written with Breuer (1893), are based squarely on observation rather than on experiment. How different from the Age of Enlightenment, whose fathers were experimentalists, the primary example being Isaac Newton.

Clearly, neuroscience has not yet attained an adequate synthesis of psychology's habit of observation and physiology's experimental vigor—rather rigor. (And perhaps vigor as well!) Can we be satisfied that the slash between mind/brain will be understood using a combination of the "new phrenology" and the modern theories of information processing applied to the nervous system now called connectionism? In answer, Professor Chomsky has written,

> Our genetic endowment provides for the growth and maturation of special mental organs . . . [and] we are fortunate to have this rich innate endowment . . . [But] the very same innate factors that provide the richness and variety of mental life . . . impose severe bounds on what the mind can achieve.*

As you have indicated, Professor Chomsky, consciousness, self-awareness, and cognition may be mysteries that can never be understood by science, neither by the methods of experimental physiology nor by observation. Following the golden clue of the genetic material, DNA, leads us only to the structures that endow humans with potential. It is the natural world we live in that provides the playground, maze, arena, forum, or battlefield for generating our actions using that potential.

Now, my reductionist scientific colleagues tend toward the philosophy of Eliminative Materialism and the computer logic of information processing. It shouldn't be a surprise that Plato's "Meno" is one of Professor Chomsky's favorite examples illustrating the innate structure of mind. In that dialogue, the specific knowledge that Socrates shows to be innate is not of geometry, syntax, semantics, or phonology, but rather the knowledge of the good. Would it be unfair to ask whether your philosophy, Professor Chomsky, can be thought of as "eliminative mentalism" with the social logic akin to Plato's theory of the good? Professor Chomsky, Meno's comment to Socrates seems to apply to you just as well. Right before the philosopher demonstrates that knowledge is inborn, he says, "In your powers over others, you seem to be like the stingray who stuns those who comes near him for my tongue is really paralyzed . . . I have given an infinite variety of lectures about cognition before now, and to many people, and, boy, I thought they were pretty good, but at this moment I cannot even say what knowing is."

CONCLUSION

Professor Noam Chomsky: [Let me first respond to] Dr. Schwartz' comment. I agree with him about one thing certainly. I think the history of science is very useful in trying to figure out what is going on here about this, and I agree with him also about the problem of the "/" in the mind/brain.

However, I think that the history of science teaches something radically different from what many contemporary biologists and, in particular, neurophysiologists have drawn from it. In fact, I think it teaches the opposite of the conclusion they draw from it. I don't think they're paying attention to the history of science, because they're kind of mesmerized with one extremely rare incident. Namely, there was one dramatic recent case of successful reductionism, as far as I know, about the only one: namely, Crick and Watson. It's true that Crick and Watson, and Pauling, and so on succeeded in giving a reductionist account of large parts of biology in terms of relatively

79

known biochemistry, but that's extremely rare in the history of science.

In fact, take the few cases that I mentioned. Take, say, Newton, the classical moment. If we followed the principle that we must have reductionism, then Newton's conclusion would be, "OK, there are no planetary orbits." Because he succeeded in demonstrating—that's what Volume II of the *Principia* is about—that you cannot explain planetary orbits or any other kind of terrestrial motion in terms of the mechanical philosophy, which is self-evident, he said, as I quoted, and as Huygens and others agreed. No person who is even sane can doubt that the mechanical philosophy is true—except that it's false! His conclusion—and he was left with this paradox. But if he followed the position of which the equivalent today is eliminative materialism, saying, "Well, let's just study the kind of thing we dogmatically assume to be true and not look at the phenomena we discover or the explanations we discover for them," he would have said: "Yes, planets don't have orbits. Kepler's laws are false. Nothing moves on the earth, because, in fact, it's all inconsistent with the mechanical philosophy," as he's shown.

Well, that's what the reductionists would have said. And in fact—that was said: if you look back at 17th-century debate, Newton's results were ridiculed by a number of very distinguished continental scientists on essentially those grounds. And Newton himself—there was some self-ridicule—he was concerned by it. It took a long time before people finally understood that that's the wrong approach.

The problem in science is not reductionism, it's unification, which is something quite different. There are different ways of looking at the world. They work to whatever extent they do, we would like to integrate them, but reduction is only one way to integrate them. And, in fact, through the course of modern science, that has rarely been true.

The question is asked; How do we get a mental event from the brain? Well, no one knows much about the slash. But how do we get planetary orbits from mechanical philosophy? Well, the answer is: We don't. Therefore, we give up the mechanical philosophy. How do we get electromagnetic phenomena from the motion of particles? The answer: We don't. Therefore, we introduce new principles, fields, Maxwell's equations, and so on and so forth, which weren't part of the earlier science. We don't say, well, there is no magnetism because it can't be explained in terms of known physics. Or, how do we get the chemical bond, let's say or the states of matter, which really weren't understood until quantum theory. How do we get them in terms of 19th-century physics? Answer: We don't.

Well, a reductionist would say: "OK, there is no chemical bond. Throw out chemistry." True, the chemists seem to be explaining all sorts of things in terms of these Kekulé molecule models, and valence, and the periodic table, but it doesn't exist. We've shown it doesn't exist because of the slash, namely, 19th-century physics is just incapable of dealing with it, therefore, we throw it out.

In fact, most of the history of science is, in fact, like that, at least as I read it. To the extent that unification has been achieved, it has not been achieved through strict reductionism, except in rare cases. It's very commonly been the case that what we think of as more the fundamental science had to be radically revised.

Let's take now the slash between the mind and the

brain. By scientific standards, at least, there are pretty successful computational theories of, say, vision, and language, and so on. They achieve some pretty surprising things. It's perfectly true, as the neurophysiologists say, that their conclusions don't mesh with what they know about the brain. Well, probably the reason for that is they just don't know the right things about the brain. That's not to say that they don't know a lot of facts. Linneaus knew lots of facts, they just happened to be the wrong facts.

During the 19th century, there was a huge discussion of what was called Prout's Law: Why do chemical elements seem to be roughly integral multiples of the atomic weight of hydrogen. There is tremendous experimentation and this and that. They had tons of phenomena, but they were the wrong phenomena, as was later discovered. It's entirely likely that the same is true in this case.

In fact, if you go back, say, fifty years, there was a huge mass of information about language. You go to the library, you'd find big fat books about all kinds of languages, but they didn't tell you a lot. The standard view among linguists was "languages can differ from one another in arbitrary ways." I'm virtually quoting, in fact. And that was a plausible conclusion from the massive data they had. They just had the wrong data.

If you look at the brain today you find the same thing. It looks as if nothing digital and computational with these weird properties that are discussed could possibly come out of this mess. Probably because you don't understand the mess. That has often been true in the past, and the way to overcome the slash is exactly the way it's always been: pursue the various approaches to understanding things, and see if you can somehow dream up a way to bring them together. You don't know what's going to have to change. You don't know if you'll be able to do it. That's been the course of science, and I think that people should not be misled by the one really striking case of reductionism.

It's perfectly true that the gap between molecules and mind is vast, but the gap between molecules and just about everything else in biology is also vast. It's striking to see how when you get above big molecules, understanding tails off very quickly, and you get into hand waving, or else just description. The problem is that, beyond the level of big molecules, you just don't understand very much; there isn't much in the way of theory.

Let's take what's called the theory of evolution. What Darwin achieved is of extraordinary importance, but there's virtually nothing of a theory there. There's nothing much to teach. You can teach population genetics and Mendel and so on, but the explanatory force is limited. There's plausible descriptive accounts of why snails get bigger shells and so on, but when you try to account for why particular organs develop, or species, and so on, all you can do is wave your hands. You say, "well, if something else had happened that wasn't functional the organism wouldn't have reproduced and would have died off." To move to more far reaching explanation, you're going to have to find something about the space of physical possibility within which selection operates. That space might be extremely narrow. For example, it might be so narrow that under the particular conditions of human evolution, there's one possibility for something with 10^{11} neurons packed into something the size of a basketball: namely, a brain that has these computational properties. I don't propose that, but something like it could turn out to be true. There might be very narrow physical possibilities of the kind that, say D'Arcy Thompson and others talked about, that create a space within which reproductive success makes a difference. Those topics are not well understood because so little is really known in any depth when you get beyond big molecules.

Just take the two examples I mentioned: the fact that children undergo puberty at a certain age, and that they achieve binocular vision at four months. Well, those are facts. Everybody assumes, without much knowledge as far as I am aware, that those things are determined by the genes somehow, but the gaps between those two facts and molecules is just as vast as the gap between generative grammar and molecules. If you take problems in embryology, like why does a chicken limb develop just the way it does, you get a lot of very interesting descriptive commentary, but very little in the way of general theory. When you get beyond proteins, understanding does tail off.

Now, what about eliminative materialism? It's a common view, that's true, among many philosophers and scientists. There are two ways of looking at eliminative materialism as far as I can see. One is that it's total gibberish until somebody tells us what matter is. Until somebody tells us what materialism is, there can't be any such thing as eliminative materialism, and *nobody* can tell you what matter is. For example, take fields. Well, they are basically mathematical objects, but physicists treat them as real because they push each other around as Roger Penrose put it. So they are real mathematical objects. Is that consistent with materialism? Every physicist says it is, but since we have no concept of matter, there is no way of answering that question. Even terrestrial motion is not consistent with what Newton thought matter was, within the mechanical philosophy. Until someone comes along and tells us what matter is, we don't know what eliminative materialism is. We can't talk about it. That's one way of looking at it.

The other way of looking at eliminative materialism is to observe the way it is actually practiced: just look at neurophysiology. You want to understand, say, undergoing puberty, look at neurophysiology. That makes about as much sense as saying to chemists 100 years ago: "You want to understand valence, look at billiard balls bumping into each other." It wasn't going to work. It might make about as much sense today as telling a neurophysiologist: "Look, you want to understand neurophysiology, look at quarks. That's where the answer is." Well, maybe, but it doesn't help a lot.

In fact, the belief that neurophysiology is even relevant to the functioning of the mind is just a hypothesis. Who knows if we're looking at the right aspects of the brain at all. Maybe there are other aspects of the brain that nobody has even dreamt of looking at yet. That's often happened in the history of science. When people say the mental is the neurophysiological at a higher level, they're being radically unscientific. We know a lot about the mental from a scientific point of view. We have explanatory theories that account for a lot of things. The belief that neurophysiology is implicated in these things *could* be true, but we have very little evidence for it. So, it's just a kind of hope; look around and you see neurons; maybe they're implicated.

The connectionist approaches that you mentioned are even stranger in my view. Connectionism is a radical abstraction from what's known about the brain and the brain sciences. Here, I think Gerald Edelman is quite right. It's a very radical abstraction. There's no reason to believe you're abstracting the right thing. There's no evidence for it. In the case of language, the evidence for connectionist models is, for the moment, about zero. The most trivial problems that have been addressed—like learning a few hundred words—have been total failures.

You can tell me about this because you surely know more about it than I do, but take the studies of nematodes, which are useful organisms because their wiring diagram is completely known. They have 300 neurons and are very simple. People know exactly the developmental pattern. There is a research group at MIT, which has been trying to figure out why the stupid little worm does the thing it does. We know entirely about its developmental pattern. We know all of its neurology, but nobody can figure out what the heck it's doing and why. They did try connectionist models and they gave them up quickly because they just abstract too far away from the physical properties of the nervous system. These are, after all, cellular structures, which interact in all kinds of ways, not just the things abstracted in synaptic connections.

My main point is, we can't be dogmatic about these things. The history of science tells us you can't be dogmatic. That's about all it tells you. It says often new understanding has come out in undreamt of ways, because systems we thought we understood, we didn't understand, and the fundamental sciences had to be radically recast. It would have been crazy to give up chemistry in the 19th century because you couldn't relate it to known physics. In fact, you had to change the known physics *radically*. Then you could bring them together, but not through reduction, through expansion if you want to give it a name, in fact, changing everything. So the reductionist moment should not be taken as a model in my opinion. The gap is real, but the way to overcome the gap is the same as in other cases. You don't know how to overcome it, you just try to understand things better and maybe you'll learn more about the brain, maybe you'll learn that you are looking at the wrong thing. Possibly the gap will be overcome or maybe we just never figure it out.

That leads to questions that George Miller raised, two of them. About not having enough capacity—I think what George said is that we may not have enough capacity—to achieve a reductionist account. The only change I'd like to make is that there's no reason to expect that a reductionist account is the true one. So I'd like to modify that and say we may not have enough capacity to achieve unification. That's quite possible. A very normal phenomenon of life is that our actions are under our control within the range of physical possibility. If somebody came along and trained a machine gun on the audience and said, "Say, 'Heil Hitler,'" and people thought he meant it, probably everybody would say, "Heil Hitler," but we know perfectly well that we don't have to. The action is under our control. We could do something else. That trivial fact is completely out of the range of any form of even bad science. Nobody has the foggiest idea of what to make of that, so, therefore, nobody pays attention to it, or people make pretenses about it. But those phenomena are as clear to us as any are, and we can't even ask the right questions about them. That's part of Descartes' point. They seem to be out of the range of our cognitive capacities, at least for now, and maybe forever.

Can we learn what's a mystery for us? It's conceivable. There's no logical contradiction in supposing we might learn what our own cognitive capacities are. So, for example, one might study problem situations and the ideas that people come up with. You take a look at the history of science, there are plenty of problem situations. People look at certain problems. Mostly they look with blank stares, nothing happens. If we take the problems raised by the Greeks, about 95 percent of them we'd look with the same blank stare that they looked at them. Every once in a while, some ideas come along, and consistently, the same ideas come to the minds of many people, usually at about the same time, or somebody happens to be first and the other people say, "Yeah, that's got to be right."

Well, the transition from the problem situation to the ideas follows a very curious path. Just as a matter of set theory, we know that there were infinitely many possible theories consistent with the facts in a problem situation. And the typical phenomenon is either we think of nothing, or else everybody more or less thinks of the same thing or at least kind of recognizes it as plausible. That indicates a high degree of structure in the cognitive system. And it is entirely possible that we could learn what that structure is. For example—I'll give you an example that's false of the kind of thing we might find. Suppose we discovered that every time we come up with a solution it's because we've been able to formulate it either as a deterministic system, or as something which involves randomness. Suppose that were what we discovered. We would then know that any system of the world which doesn't fall within that bound is a mystery to us. We could discover something like that. I'm not suggesting that's the right one, but we could discover something like that. So maybe there's a way to study the bounds of our understanding. At the moment, all I think we can do is be descriptive. Say, look, here are an awful lot of things where we can't even think of the right questions, let alone the right answers.

About George's other point that, namely, he and Jerry Bruner and I have all been kind of grumpy about the course of cognitive science and have said that the subject's kidnapped, one could make an unkind comment: namely, take a look at our ages and think what people of our age tend to say about their children and the course that they're pursuing. But let me put that aside. In my opinion at least, in the specific empirical areas of the so-called cognitive sciences, some have been doing pretty reasonably, like the study of vision and the study of language and so on. The general conception of what it's all about in my opinion is badly wrong, and has inherited all kinds of errors and, in fact, I think has not reached the level of the 17th century in many respects for reasons I mentioned.

Well, Akeel's questions would take much more time to answer than I could if I had the time, or knew what to answer, which I don't. On the question of the lexicon and perspectives and accessibility to consciousness, what he says seems to me plausible—if I understood it—but I think there's another possibility we might think about. In the case of simple lexical meaning, we know very little. You take a look at a word like "London" or "table" or "house" or "dog" or something, and try to figure out what you know about that word, and you find that it is so radically beyond anything that's ever been described that you're just caught up in a big descriptive problem in the first place. Now we don't have anything much in the way of theory about these things. There is no theory to speak of about agent's perspectives, which, in my view, is the right way to look at it. As a result, we are just stuck with descriptive commentary like most of evolutionary biology. When you have just descriptive commentary about yourselves, it is all accessible to consciousness. What else could it be? If we had a theory about agent's perspectives, we might discover that it is not accessible to us any more than the principles that are involved in that slightly more complex sentence that I mentioned are accessible to us. That we don't know. Where things seem accessible, it may well be because we just don't understand enough. And we're just trying to get a sense of what the descriptive phenomena are for the first time. This is a topic that's rarely been studied. I think George Miller's work is some of the first study of it, and we all know it just barely touches the surfaces. You can see when you think about even the trivial examples I mentioned.

On the other matter, do we confirm or refute the Turing Test by considering the possibility of a machine that duplicates our finite behavior? Well, I'm not convinced. Let's try an analog. We breathe. Roughly speaking what happens is air comes into the nose and carbon dioxide goes out after a lot of things go on. So there is an input-output system, air to carbon dioxide. We could get a machine that duplicates that completely by some crazy mechanism. Would the machine be breathing? Well, no, the machine would not be breathing for trivial reasons. Breathing is a thing that humans do, therefore, the machine isn't breathing. Is it a good model of humans? Well, that we'd look at and see if it teaches us anything about humans. If it does, it's a good model of humans. If it doesn't teach us anything about humans, send it to Hume's flames.

It seems to me exactly the same is true when we turn to thought and intelligence. Let's say somebody could come along with a chess-playing program that behaved exactly like Kasparov, made exactly the moves he would every time. Would it be playing chess? Well, no, just as in the case of "breathing." Playing chess is something that people do. Kasparov has a brain, but his brain doesn't play chess. If we asked, "Does Kasparov's brain play chess," the answer is no, any more than my legs take a walk. It's a *trivial* point. It's not an interesting point to discuss. My legs don't take a walk, my brain doesn't play chess or understand English. Just for the same reason that a submarine doesn't swim. Swimming is something that fish do. If we want to extend the metaphor to submarines, we could say they do. English happened to pick a different metaphor, but these are not substantive questions. A machine that duplicated the air-to-carbon dioxide exchange would not be breathing for trivial reasons, just as if a robot sticks a knife into somebody's heart, it's not murdering him. Robots can't murder. That's something humans do. For these reasons, the questions just don't mean anything.

Therefore, it doesn't seem to me possible to refute the Turing Test this way. I think Turing was right. Remember what Turing said. He said, look, the question whether a machine can think is too meaningless to deserve discussion. It's like asking in 1900 whether an airplane flies. It's not a meaningful question. It flies if you want to call that flying. It doesn't fly if you don't want to call that flying. It's just like asking, "Does my brain think?" That's not the way we talk English, but if you want to change the language you could say it. The same is true about this breathing device or about machines thinking and so on.

What Turing suggested is, let's drop the question of what thinking is, and let's try to create models of intelligence, computational models of intelligence. That's perfectly reasonable. That's like 250 years ago, de Vaucanson saying let's construct an automaton that does things kind of like a duck, because maybe it will teach us something about ducks. Turing's point was maybe this will teach us something about thinking. Well, he also said that maybe 50 years from now we will have just changed our language, and we'll talk about that as thinking as we talk about airplanes flying. But nothing substantive will have happened, just the decision to use a metaphor, like deciding to say that submarines set sail. It doesn't mean anything, and we're not confused into thinking it.

In my opinion, all the discussion that's gone on for the last ten years about, say, John Searle's Chinese room and so on, or how do we empirically decide whether computers play chess, it seems to me just like asking: Does the brain think? Do my legs take a walk? If a rock fell off a roof and shattered someone's skull, did the rock murder him? It's the same kind of question. These are not meaningful questions. We should drop them and just look at the serious questions like whether simulation teaches us anything. If it does, good; if it doesn't, throw it out. Simulation that doesn't teach us anything is useless.

Take the whole business about chess-playing programs, which as Herbert Simon once put it, I think, is the "drosophila of cognitive science," the idea around which everything converges. He's sort of right descriptively, but that tells you exactly where the field has gone off from the first moment. There are few projects less interesting, scientifically, than a chess-playing program. For one thing because chess playing is not an interesting topic to study; right now, it's unlikely to help us learn anything about human beings. It's as if we didn't understand how people walk, and someone said, "Let's figure out how they pole vault." That just wouldn't be a sane scientific endeavor. Let's first figure out how they move one leg in front of the other, then maybe someday we'll get to pole vaulting. Playing chess is something way out on the margins of what people do—that's why it's a game. It's too remote from what we understand to make any sense to study. Furthermore, from the very first moment it became clear that the way to win at chess was to deviate radically from the way human beings do it and to use the capacities of computers. That just means it's rotten simulation. If Carnegie Tech's computer program can beat Kasparov, that's about as interesting as the fact that a bulldozer can lift more than some weight lifter. Maybe. Who cares? It doesn't teach you anything about the weight lifter, and it's of no scientific interest. In fact, about its only interest is to take the fun out of playing chess as far as I can see. Now the fact that a huge amount of effort and money from the National Science Foundation—I hope not the Russell Sage Foundation—has gone into this, simply shows how conceptual errors have misled the field, in my opinion. We should be aware of that.

Dr. Wanner: Let us thank Dr. Anshen for convening the meeting. Ruth, would you like to have the last word:

Dr. Anshen: I want also to thank the discussants and, of course, Noam Chomsky and Charles Ryskamp. I only want to remind all of us that the poets have been ignored, but Professor Chomsky has intimated as a hint, perhaps, that they, the poets, are a relevant example of the mystery of the creative process, of mind/brain/spirit, even thought, morals, consciousness, wisdom, and language. Let us take the poet Rimbaud. I'll say it first in French; some of you will understand it. *"C'est faux de dire, je pense; on devrait dire, on me pense."* Now I translate: "It is false to say, I think; one must say, it thinks me." This mystery of "it" is the source, in my opinion, of creativity, whether in art, music, science, philosophy. We must reverence the mystery of creativity. Shall this mystery ever be revealed to us?

Unknown speaker: I hope not.

Dr. Wanner: Thank you all very much for coming.

BIOGRAPHICAL NOTES

RUTH NANDA-ANSHEN, PH.D., Fellow of the Royal Society of Arts of London, founded, plans, and edits, several distinguished series of books, including World Perspectives Religious Perspectives, Credo Perspectives, Perspectives in Humanism, the Science of Culture Series, the Tree of Life Series, and Convergence. She has exerted remarkable influence through her worldwide lectures, her writings, her ability to attract a most important group of contributors to these series, underlying the unitary principle of all reality, and particularly through her close association with many of the great scientists and thinkers of this century, from Whitehead, Einstein, Bohr, and Heisenberg to Rabi, Tillich, Chomsky, and Wheeler. Dr. Anshen's book *Anatomy of Evil*, a study in the phenomenology of evil, demonstrates the interrelationship between good and evil. She is also the author of *Biography of an Idea*, and the recent volume *Morals Equals Manners*. Dr. Anshen is a member of the American Philosophical Association, the History of Science Society, the International

Philosophical Society, and the Metaphysical Society of America. Founder of the Anshen Transdisciplinary Lectureships in Art, Science, and the Philosophy of Culture at the Frick Collection.

Dr. Eric Wanner, President of the Russell Sage Foundation, New York City.

Noam Chomsky; Professor of Linguistics and Philosophy; Massachusetts Institute of Technology.

Akeel Bilgrami; Professor of Philosophy, Columbia University.

James Schwartz; Professor of Neuro-Biology, College of Physicians and Surgeons, Columbia University.

George A. Miller, Professor of Psychology, Princeton University.